RALPH GARLICK

RALPH REYNOLDS GARLICK (1876-1931).

RALPH GARLICK
1876-1931

A Stratford Story

Richard Mallison

BREWIN BOOKS

First published by
Brewin Books Ltd, 56 Alcester Road,
Studley, Warwickshire B80 7LG in 2019
www.brewinbooks.com

© Richard Mallison 2019

All rights reserved.

ISBN: 978-1-85858-704-2

The moral right of the author has been asserted.

A Cataloguing in Publication Record
for this title is available from the British Library.

Typeset in Haarlemmer MT Std
Printed in Great Britain by
Hobbs The Printers Ltd.

Contents

Introduction vi
Prologue vii

Part 1: Stratford & Oxford

1. The Garlicks of Stratford-upon-Avon 3
2. King Edward VI School: (I) The Headmaster 11
3. King Edward VI School: (II) The All-Rounder..............17
4. King Edward VI School: (III) The Scholar 24
5. Pembroke College, Oxford 30

Part 2: India

6. The Steel Frame of India 39
7. Turbulent Times 56
8. Lethal Encounter 63
9. Depart with Honour 70
10. Remembrance 80

Garlick Family Tree..83
Notes and References 84
List of Illustrations 86
Bibliography 88
Acknowledgements 90
Index..93

Introduction

Every seven years the student population of a school entirely changes yet the ethos, traditions and legends endure, passed on through the generations by a process of collective memory.

Each year the K.E.S. Archive publishes an Alumni Roll, listing the years of attendance of those students for whom records exist. Flicking through the pages, amongst the thousands of former scholars, one comes across familiar names whose exploits have been immortalised in the names of School Houses, buildings or Speech Day prizes. A few stories are well known: "Rex" Warneford, recipient of the Victoria Cross; Richard Spender, the World War II poet. Other names, less frequently heard, have histories not so readily recalled. Into that category falls Ralph Reynolds Garlick.

Richard Mallison's fascinating book charts Ralph's progress from relatively humble beginnings in Stratford-upon-Avon, a self-proclaimed *"quiet town of spectators rather than players",* to the upper echelons of the legal system in the British Raj, and his shocking assassination, a victim of the tumultuous times that engulfed the country as it moved towards independence. Mallison, a retired school teacher, writes with evident affection for and understanding of this former Old Boy who might easily have been one of his own charges.

Ralph was a pioneer: the first Head Boy at King Edward VI School under a great reforming Headmaster; and a member of the first cohort to join the Indian Civil Service based on merit not patronage. Nevertheless, Mallison's meticulous research reveals those poignant, family details which help to convey so vividly Ralph's character. One of seven siblings brought up in a busy, musical household, he was purposeful, thoughtful and liberal. He left grammar school and Oxford possessing a keen sense of duty and justice. The brutal murder of this fundamentally modest and shy man occasioned an outpouring of anger and grief across the globe.

Mallison's brilliant eye for the telling detail enables him to bring to life the historical facts surrounding an individual whilst emphasising their contextual significance in an age apparently so different from our own.

For example, one experiences as if at first hand that particular mixture of trepidation and excitement as Ralph stands, on the deck of the *"Persia"* one cold winter's night. Setting off from Tilbury on a three-week voyage, he will start a new life in India in Christmas 1900…

Bennet Carr
Headmaster, King Edward VI School

Prologue

When I joined the staff of King Edward VI in the late 1960s the Guildhall, built circa 1420, was the core of the school, drawing in daily a steady stream of boys and masters for a multiplicity of purposes. Its two principal spaces were the Lower Hall, which housed the non-fiction library, and the Upper Hall known as "Big School". Although still serving principally as a classroom – as it had done continuously since the young William Shakespeare had attended in the early 1570s – Big School also had a variety of other uses: as an examinations room for the senior school; as a venue for school drama productions (again, echoes of Shakespeare); for the end-of-term whole-school assemblies (with the potential for a heavy loss of life in the event of a fire!); and as a venue for dinners to celebrate the retirement of long-serving members of staff.

Big School's two most striking features were (and still are) its massive beams and the rows of eighteenth century heavy oak desks. Less conspicuous, yet eye-catching nevertheless, was the handsome oak and bronze tablet which was affixed to its eastern wall. How and why the tablet came to be there was only sketchily contained within its inscription. My curiosity was piqued but the opportunity for further investigation proved elusive – until now. More than fifty years on since my earliest encounters with the tablet I have been able to piece together the Garlick story, and what an absorbing one it has turned out to be.

The Garlick Memorial tablet (centre of photograph) in its original location on the eastern wall of Big School circa 2006. [By kind permission of Mr Tony Bird].

Part 1

STRATFORD & OXFORD

"A complete and generous education (is) that which fits a man to perform justly, skilfully and magnanimously all the offices both public and private of peace and war"

John Milton, Of Education, 1644

Chapter 1

The Garlicks of Stratford-upon-Avon

Ralph (pronounced RAY-FF not the more usual RALL-FF) Reynolds Garlick was born in Stratford in 1876, the sixth of seven surviving children of George and Caroline (a son and two daughters had died before Ralph was born). Ralph was a second generation Stratfordian. His mother Caroline (née Hancox) was born in 1836 into a farming family at Snitterfield, a village just outside Stratford. By 1861 Caroline had left the farm and was assisting her widowed aunt who was trading as a Grocer and Tallow Chandler at 28 Wood Street, but a short distance from number 45 which at a later date was to become the Garlick family home. At the time her husband-to-be and Ralph's father was living in nearby West Street with his younger, and as yet unmarried, sister Mary who also carried the family middle name of Reynolds.

Although uncommon as a forename in the wider world, Reynolds appears frequently as a middle name among Ralph's immediate family, both male and female and across several generations. One source posits a link with William Shakespeare, suggesting that William Reynolds (1575-1633), a friend of the playwright who also lived in Chapel Street just four places away from New Place, was an ancestor. Reynolds, who was a leading landowner but was also said to be a recusant – a Roman Catholic who refused to attend the services of the Church of England – was left two marks (roughly £1.30 in today's coinage) in Shakespeare's will to buy a mourning ring. The claim is an interesting one but cannot be corroborated by his present-day family. An alternative, if more prosaic, explanation is that Ralph was named after his paternal grandmother (see Garlick family tree page 83).

Ralph's father George, though he was to have an enormous impact on the town, did not hail from Stratford but was born in Lechlade in Gloucestershire in 1837 and moved to the town when in his early twenties. Following in his father's footsteps he became a teacher at the British School[1] which had been founded in 1824 in rooms at the back of the Rother Market Chapel, where he was joined by his sister Mary. On his marriage to Caroline in 1862 he set up home in Rother Street and embarked on a life's work in music. Initially this was as a music teacher but, in the early 1870s, the family, which now included four children, moved to 45 Wood Street from where he began to trade as a seller of musical instruments as well as providing tuition in music.[2]

George Garlick's contribution to the musical life of the town, both vocal and instrumental, was immense. As a music teacher by profession the number of young Stratfordians taught music by him was said to have *"run into thousands."* For years he was conductor of the Stratford-upon-Avon Choral Society. At his death in 1910 among the many tributes paid it was said that *"he was known to everyone in the town, and in all musical circles his presence was welcome and highly appreciated."* He was a lifelong member and a deacon of the Congregational Church in Rother Street, where he was also leader of the choir for over forty years and sometime organist. Several of his family followed in his musical footsteps, two of his daughters and his youngest son as teachers and/or performers, and a grandson as a piano tuner. Long after he ceased teaching at the British School he continued to be heavily involved in its

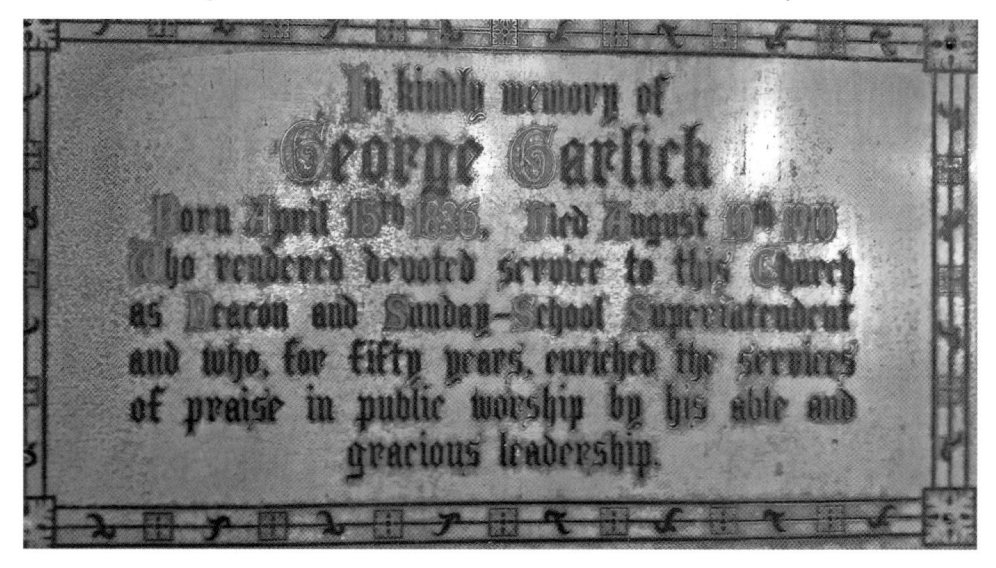

The memorial tablet to Ralph's father, George Garlick, in the United Reformed Church (formally the Congregational Church) in Rother Street.

1. The Garlicks of Stratford-upon-Avon

affairs through weekly visits. He also found time in a busy life to serve as Deputy Registrar of Marriages. He was buried alongside his wife Caroline (who died in 1908) at Stratford's Evesham Road Cemetery.

Following George's death the music business in Wood Street passed to the next generation of Garlicks when his youngest son Charles assumed control and continued trading as *"George Garlick & Son"*. The property was therefore in the possession of the Garlick family for over sixty years. It also has a claim to interest as one of the town's important timbered buildings. Local historian Dr Robert Bearman describes 45 Wood Street as *"a fine specimen of early sixteenth century work, unlike so many in Stratford, which has succeeded in retaining its ground-floor jetty and nearly all its original timbers."*[3] An earlier, and slightly more technical, description of the house was published in 1925 when Charles Garlick was still in occupation:

> *"A good example of a very early wood-framed house with simple close timbering and massive beams and posts. The corner posts have pilasters of simple design cut out of the solid, and have plain curved brackets mortised into their upper ends. The rest of the overhang is carried on prolongations of the floor-joists. The whole of the timbers are original, only necessary repairs to them having been done, and no alterations made. As a whole, the structure resembles the Almshouses and is of the same period."*[4]

All three of Ralph's brothers attended K.E.S. (the initials by which King Edward VI School is known), though none of them made a particular mark on the School. George (born 1864) was admitted in 1872 and left in 1879, after which he became an apprentice to an ironmonger. Later he moved to Birmingham to follow the same trade before becoming the steward of the Liberal Club in Aston. Walter (born 1872) joined K.E.S. in 1884 at the same time as Ralph but left twenty months later. He became a carpenter but appears to have left Stratford sometime in the mid 1890s and died in Mauritius in 1899, probably in Army service. The youngest brother, Charles, attended K.E.S. between 1888 and 1893 and on leaving joined the family business. He became the sole proprietor on his father's death in 1910 and continued to run the Wood Street music shop until 1931. He was a member of the fledgling *Old Stratfordian Club* and attended its annual Supper in January 1913 when he formed part of a *"small string band (which) discoursed three admirable selections."* Later that year Charles was the member of a string quartet which played old English airs during a meeting of the Shakespeare

45 Wood Street circa 1930. The name GARLICK can be discerned above the shop to the left. *[By kind permission of the Shakespeare Birthplace Trust]*.

1. The Garlicks of Stratford-upon-Avon

Club. He lived on to perpetuate the name of Garlick in Stratford for several more decades, married to Edith but without children. The last of the Garlick Old Edwardians died in 1957 and was buried at the Evesham Road Cemetery.

Of Ralph's three older sisters two remained in Stratford all their lives and, together with his brother Charles, maintained for him a familial link with the town. The oldest, Elizabeth Reynolds (born 1864), became a teacher of pianoforte and in 1895 married the recently-widowed Frederick Eason who owned the gents' outfitters next door at Nos 46 and 47 Wood Street. Gertrude Helen (born 1866 and known as Nell), had moved to London with her husband Joseph Perkin, an architect and surveyor, but during a visit to Stratford in 1925 was killed in a car crash on the Fosse Way near to Shipston-on-Stour. (She is buried in her parents' grave at the Evesham Road Cemetery). Elsie (born 1873 and the nearest to Ralph in age) was engaged with music all her life; at ten years old she started to play the piano at the Sunday School held in the Congregational Chapel and sixty years later was still playing at Sunday services in the town. She and her husband William Howe, the headmaster of Grove House School in Greenhill Street, were active members of the Stratford Choral and Orchestral Society for many years.[5] Elsie was in popular demand as an accompanist at their concerts and when she stepped down in 1928 she was made an honorary Vice-President in recognition *"for the many years of unselfish and loyal devotion she had generously given in the interests of the Stratford-upon-Avon Choral Society."*[6]

Gertrude (Nell) Garlick (Mrs Perkin).   *Elsie Garlick (Mrs Howe).*

There is every reason to believe that Ralph enjoyed a secure and contented childhood. The moderately-spacious and well-appointed family home was in the very centre of the town on its main thoroughfare. His parents were highly visible and well-regarded members of the community and Ralph is likely to have been in receipt of at least a modicum of mothering from his three older sisters. The two brothers either side of him in age are likely companions, though his friendships with other boys in the town were to prove the most enduring. Robert Mansell Smith (b. 1875), who lived immediately opposite Ralph at Nos 3 & 4 Wood Street where his father ran a drapery business, would go on to become mayor of the town (twice) and was destined to play a prominent role in the events held in commemoration of Ralph nearly fifty years later. Other friends lived close-by:

Aubrey Deer (b. 1876) lived in Rother Street; Horace Wiltshire (b. 1875) in Arden Street; Harold Colbourne (b. 1873) whose father was the proprietor of the Red Horse Hotel in Bridge Street; and Frank Page (b. 1875) whose mother was the licensee of the Garrick Inn in High Street.

The bond between the five boys was reinforced when all became contemporaries at the grammar school and is captured in a photograph from 1891 (below); it shows the pig roast that was held in mid-January on an ice-bound River Avon with the Clopton Bridge as a backcloth. Ralph, Aubrey, Horace, Harold and Frank, smartly turned out in their school jackets and caps, can be clearly seen among the group of onlookers on the left of the picture. The winter of 1890/91 was among the severest of the century and Stratfordians had

A pig is roasted on the River Avon during the Great Frost of 1891. Clopton Bridge is in the background. Ralph is among the group of boys from K.E.S. on the left of the picture. The photograph was owned by George Rose (K.E.S. 1890-95), whose father was the proprietor of the Swans Nest Hotel and the "Pleasure Boat Keeper". [By kind permission of the Shakespeare Birthplace Trust].

flocked to the Avon attracted by the prospect of *"an ice carnival such as is seldom witnessed in this country."* The fire had been built on planks laid across the ice, though *"the heat was so great that the surrounding ice was largely reduced to slush."* A tent had been erected on the nearby island and *"at dinner time numerous townspeople dined in the marquee under these novel circumstances, the pork being pronounced excellent."* The five school friends could well have been among the many skaters (*"upwards of a thousand"*) who took to the ice that afternoon, while a local string band played on the river bank in the Bancroft Gardens.[7]

Ralph's boyhood pleasures were not confined to Stratford town, however, as the Garlick children are known to have stayed at their maternal grandparents' farm at nearby Snitterfield. This was a sizeable enterprise of 210 acres and employed three men and two boys. Ralph must surely have relished his brief sojourns in the Warwickshire countryside.

The pupil rolls which would identify Ralph's junior school are not to hand, but given the family's close affinity with Stratford's Congregational Church there can be little doubt that he, together with his siblings, would have attended the British School in Rother Street where his father had been appointed as teacher some twenty years earlier. When the time came for Ralph to enter the grammar school he would surely have done so with a fair degree of confidence. His older brother George, who had already completed his education there, would have been able to advise him on the school's customs and practices, on what to expect from the black-gowned masters, and on the studies he would have been required to undertake. The fact that he would be joined at, or around, the same time by all four of his childhood friends would have eased his transition to senior school. In short, Ralph had little to fear and much to look forward to as he made ready to enter King Edward VI School.

Chapter 2
King Edward VI School:
(I) The Headmaster

Ralph joined King Edward VI in April 1884 but his prospects at the outset would not have seemed particularly promising as the school was not in best order at the time. It had known four different headmasters in the previous ten years and at the time of his admission there were fewer than forty pupils and a staff of two masters. The opening of Trinity College further along Church Street in 1872 and which quickly gained in popularity had been

SURNAME.	CHRISTIAN NAME.	DATE OF BIRTH.	DATE OF ADMISSION.
183. Garlick	Walter Hancock	26th Oct 1871	April 1884
184. Garlick	Ralph Reynolds	14th Feb. 1876	Ap 1884
185. Colbourne	William Harold Gardner	5th Nov 1873	Sept 1884
186. Pratt	Herbert George	4 June 1875	Sep. 1884

Ralph's entry (no. 184) in the K.E.S. Admissions Register. Those either side are of his brother Walter (no. 183) and of his boyhood friend Harold Colbourne (no. 185).

(from the grammar school perspective) an unwelcome development. K.E.S. was struggling and desperately in need of energetic and visionary leadership. Fortunately it materialized in the form of the Rev. de Courcy Laffan with a double-first in Classics from Oxford, ordained in 1882 and previously senior Classics master at Derby School. He was appointed to the headship in January 1885, a few months after Ralph's admission, and his tenure in office was to match almost exactly Ralph's years as a pupil.

During his ten years at K.E.S. Laffan brought about a much-needed transformation in all areas of school life. He widened the curriculum, built new classrooms, re-invigorated the boarding department, introduced organised games and Physical Education and set up Music and Debating Societies. He established the Guild Preparatory School under the headmastership of Mr W.E. Carey (Cavendish College, Cambridge) with the express purpose of supplying *"a continuous stream of well-trained candidates for admission to the Grammar School."* Early results were favourable and in the first few years a number of the prep school boys had moved up to K.E.S. He sought to strengthen the teaching side of the school by recruiting additional staff (with close attention paid to their suitability and qualification) and was assiduous in persuading the Governors to increase staff remuneration. At the same time he was not afraid to remove obstacles to progress. In 1892 he reported to the Governors on *"the growing inefficiency of our late Mathematical Master, a dissatisfaction the source of which has now been removed by his departure from the School."*

It was not only substantive innovations that he engineered; quite modest changes to the way in which the school was run also fell within his purview. Within a few months of his arrival, *"as a help towards effective work,"* he had opened the school during the evenings *"in order that all boys who wished to do so might have an opportunity of preparing their lessons in undisturbed quiet."* Given that Ralph's home at 45 Wood Street had to accommodate three adults and several offspring, and that his father conducted a flourishing music business from the property, it would be most surprising if Ralph was not among the large number of boys who availed themselves of this opportunity for some quiet end-of-day study.

Until the 1870s K.E.S. had not been a boarding establishment, though during the headmastership of the Rev. Joseph Greene (1735-1772) it is known from correspondence that Master West, son of the Hon. James West of Alscot Park near Stratford, had lived with the headmaster. There may have been others accommodated in a similar way but none are recorded. In 1877, however, the Governors purchased the property which lay opposite New Place Gardens in Chapel Lane and this became School House open to boarders. The initial take-up was not encouraging and when Laffan arrived in 1885 there were only two boarders. However, thanks to his vision, with the unstinting support of the Governors, and under his wife's caring stewardship, the number of boarders surged. By 1887 there were six boarders, then eleven, and by 1892 there were twenty boarders and six resident assistant masters in School House. Testimonials from parents, though they need to be treated with caution, reinforce the view that the boarding arrangements offered by the School were finding favour well beyond the confines of Stratford. A Mr and Mrs Marriott Hall from Worksop wrote: *"The great care and kindness of Mrs Laffan…has had a very marked influence on their sons, and they have every confidence in recommending this to the notice of parents."* From Major Flood Page in Sydenham: *"It seems to me that Mrs Laffan aims at making the boys committed to their charge as happy and as comfortable as they were at home."*

That a Garlick should have boarded, given that the family lived a mere 200 yards from the School gate (and nearer than William Shakespeare in nearby Henley Street!) is surprising, but one did so. Ralph's younger brother Charles is identified as a boarder in the School records, though they are silent on when and for how long. While, as a Burgess of the Town, George Garlick would have been exempt from the payment of entrance fees, he would of course have been liable for boarding fees. The most plausible explanation for Charles as a boarder is that accommodation at Wood Street was at a premium and his absence will have eased the pressure. (During the 1890s a third adult, George's sister Lucianne, was living at No. 45). Or it might be that Charles and/or his parents could see the benefits to be had from a boarding arrangement.

It was also during Laffan's stewardship that a major programme of restoration was carried out to the old Guild buildings. His drive to secure additional accommodation together with his vision and assertiveness were instrumental in persuading Charles Flower, an Old Boy and benefactor, to fund the restoration of the medieval buildings in the early 1890s (see next chapter).

Ralph was in only his third year at K.E.S. when Laffan made a discovery on the school site which was to enable the Town to augment its already-sizeable collection of historical records. While investigating a staircase which led from the Armoury to the end of Big School he encountered a locked door

The Rev. de Courcy Laffan, Headmaster of King Edward VI School 1885-95.

2. King Edward VI School: (I) The Headmaster

which, in the absence of a key, he forced open. Inside what is now known as the Muniment Room he discovered a considerable quantity of deeds and documents. These were removed and deposited with the Shakespeare Birthplace Trust whose Librarian, Richard Savage, scrutinized 240 apprenticeship indentures, 871 bonds of indemnity plus miscellaneous documents and volumes. Although only five of the apprentice indentures were of Shakespeare's time they were of special significance not only for the Town but also to the School itself since all five indentures had been executed by Alexander Aspinall who had been Headmaster from 1582 until 1629. He was also a friend of the adult Shakespeare, an alderman of the borough and several times appointed deputy town clerk. One signature identified by Savage was that of "Richard Hathway" which, if confirmed as being that of Shakespeare's brother-in-law, would make it of particular interest. Savage reported that the whole collection *"bears autographs of persons of interest in Stratford's history, and likewise furnishes us with information as to some of the trades ancientedly carried on, but which have long ceased to be a Stratford industry."* The find was a noteworthy event for both the School and the Town Archive.

It was Ralph's good fortune that for the whole of the time he was at K.E.S. he was under the progressive headship of the Rev. Laffan. By the time of the latter's departure in 1895 to become Principal of Cheltenham College, K.E.S. was said by one educational journal to occupy *"no less a place than first among all the smaller public schools in England."* Small perhaps but appreciably bigger than it had been a decade earlier with one hundred boys now on the roll, twenty of them boarders, and seven full-time members of staff, mostly from Oxford or Cambridge.

Laffan had flourished at Stratford, a relatively small establishment seriously in need of the vigorous leadership which he was well equipped and most willing to provide. In contrast Cheltenham was a well-established and larger public school which proved to be far less receptive to his reforming zeal. He resigned his post after four years, leaving headmastership for good, and became Rector of St. Stephen's, Walbrook in 1899.

By then he had already begun what was to become a close association with the international Olympic movement. He had always been a keen sportsman (while at Merton College Oxford he had rowed in the college eight) and had developed physical training and athletic sports while at K.E.S. However, he saw not just the physical benefits of sporting activity but held strongly that it was through physical exercise that *"man came to know himself better, and that this in turn would lead to the establishment of the Brotherhood of Man."* This conviction chimed well with Baron Pierre de Coubetin's own emerging ideas. At a Congress of the recently-formed International Olympic Committee (IOC) in 1897 Laffan represented the Headmasters' Conference (the association of headmasters of the English public schools). After meeting Laffan and hearing his address to the Congress, de Coubetin recognized in him a kindred spirit and a friendship developed between the two men which was to become *"profound and stable."* Laffan became a member of the IOC in 1897 and in 1905 he was central to the founding of the British Olympic Association (BOA). He was the Association's first Honorary Secretary from 1905 until his death in 1927.

But Laffan never forgot Stratford or the School and returned frequently. In May 1905, for example, he was the *"special preacher"* at the formal opening and dedication of a new organ in the Guild Chapel. He also attended Old Boys' Dinners and Speech Days, notably in 1919 at the first Speech Day after the war (and *his* last) when he presented the prizes.

Chapter 3

King Edward VI School: (II) The All-Rounder

The absence of pupil-specific records at K.E.S. in the 1880s/90s makes it virtually impossible to track an individual's progress or achievements. This deficiency was partially remedied when in 1893 the first issue of the school magazine, *The Stratfordian*, was published. Since it was written in part by the boys themselves and had much to say about their many and varied activities, the early issues of the magazine offer a valuable window into school life in the closing years of the nineteenth century. Ralph, now in the Senior School, was one such pupil contributor.

What stands out is the range of his interests and the high standard he invariably achieved in each. They included drama, sport, societies, composition and, above all, scholarship. Ralph played a prominent part in plays which since 1886 had formed part of the Annual Speech Day programme. In December 1892, in front of *"some four hundred spectators"* (including *"the neighbouring gentry"*) Ralph was cast as Creon in an excerpt from *Oedipus at Coloneus*. *The Stratfordian* reported that *"the brunt of the acting was borne by R.R. Garlick and G.R. Talbot (as Oedipus), to whom the premier honours must undoubtedly be assigned."* The report continued: *"Garlick acquitted himself admirably, and had evidently fully entered into the spirit of his very difficult part."* He was involved again the following year, his last, when he took the role of Hercules in the Greek play *Alcestis*.

On the sporting front Ralph was a member of the K.E.S. 1st XV for his last three seasons and had already earned his colours by 1892. As a front row forward his efforts were less visible than those of the more glitzy backs but he

KING · EDWARD · VI · SCHOOL,
STRATFORD-ON-AVON.

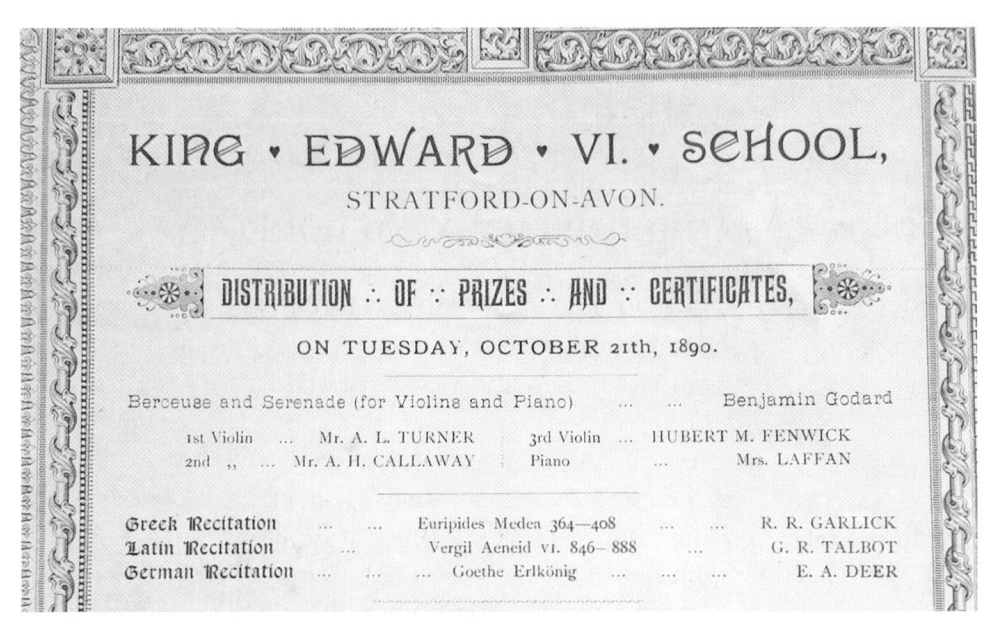

DISTRIBUTION ∴ OF ∴ PRIZES ∴ AND ∴ CERTIFICATES,

ON TUESDAY, OCTOBER 21th, 1890.

Berceuse and Serenade (for Violins and Piano) ... ... Benjamin Godard

1st Violin ... Mr. A. L. TURNER	3rd Violin ... HUBERT M. FENWICK	
2nd ,, ... Mr. A. H. CALLAWAY	Piano ... Mrs. LAFFAN	

Greek Recitation ...	Euripides Medea 364—408 ...	R. R. GARLICK
Latin Recitation ...	Vergil Aeneid vi. 846–888 ...	G. R. TALBOT
German Recitation ...	... Goethe Erlkönig ...	E. A. DEER

Prize Giving 1890.

gained recognition nevertheless. He was described in one match report as being *"conspicuous in the front rank"* while in a report of the match against King Henry VIII School, Coventry played in October 1893 reference is made to *"the strenuous exertion of Garlick."* His end-of-season profile states: *"Hardworking forward; very valuable in the scrum and line-out."* In what was probably his last appearance on a rugby pitch in November 1898 he turned out for the Old Boys XV which beat the School XV.

While rugby at the time appears not to have had a permanent home (matches were played on different parts of Seven Meadows) cricketers were more fortunate in that the school field was on the opposite side of the river from the Bancroft Gardens and was rented from the Town Council. Ralph was opening batsman for the K.E.S. 2nd XI but did not overtire the scorers.

Ralph also featured in *The Stratfordian* as a contributor. In the second issue of July 1893 under the heading *"The Restoration of the School"* he gives a highly positive account of the work so far undertaken. Pedagogue's House, which had been in a distressed state for some time, had now undergone major refurbishment. The internal alterations had created three new badly-needed classrooms, one on the ground floor and two above, which Ralph pronounced *"exceedingly pleasant"*. Work on the medieval Guild building was still ongoing but in the next issue (April 1894) Ralph was able to report that it was no longer marred by *"its prosaic frontage glaring with the red doors of the engine house* (the Guildhall had been housing the town fire engine!) *and plumber's shop* (later Sergeant's lodge)" and *"by the tumble-down erections at the rear."* The last had been removed and the site grassed over. The major alterations which had been undertaken to the interior of the building (thereby creating still more space for use by the school) included the removal of the partition in Big School which divided it into the Mathematics Room in the southern half and the Latin Room in the northern. A new staircase leading up from the vestibule outside the Guildhall had been built to provide the principal access to the upper rooms. A key phase of the work had been the removal of the disfiguring layer of roughcast which had covered the exterior of the Guildhall since the previous century to reveal the original black and white timbers. The windows down the Church Street side of Big School were re-designed and enlarged at the same time.

While Ralph was able to enthuse about the state of the medieval school buildings once the restoration work was complete he is likely to have been far less sanguine about the disruption caused to the members of the school, staff and boys alike, while the work was ongoing, especially from the start of the Michaelmas term (1892) to the end of the Easter term (1893). In his Annual Report to the Governors, Laffan states that during this period *"at no time were all the rooms in the School buildings available for School purposes."* Indeed, for the first five weeks of the Michaelmas term *"we were obliged to carry out the work of the Lower School at the Coffee Tavern in Bridge Street, marching the boys to and fro for the purpose."* Even after the staff and boys were able to enter the school buildings *"change after change had to be made after one classroom after another had either to be re-occupied after restoration, or evacuated to enable it to take place."* Cognizant of the disruption, the Examiner in his end of year Report was moved to comment that although the year *"had been a very broken one for school work"* he was *"surprised to find that the excellence of the work seemed in no way to have been impaired."*

A by-product of the restoration was, according to the Headmaster, *"an increase in the number of visitors applying for admission to the School."* This led the Governors to put in place arrangements which enabled the Guildhall to offer itself as a (part-time) *"visitor attraction"*. The July 1894 issue of *The Stratfordian* reported:

Below: King Edward VI School from Scholars Lane circa 1885. The fire engine was housed behind the double doors. With a disfiguring layer of roughcast, this is how Ralph would have known the Guildhall in his early years as a pupil. [Photographer Douglas McNeille. By kind permission of the Shakespeare Birthplace Trust].

Right: King Edward VI School from Church Street circa 1894, as Ralph would have known it in his final years. Restoration work had stripped away the roughcast to reveal the original black and white timber. It would be another five years before the roughcast on the adjoining almshouses was removed. [By kind permission of the Shakespeare Birthplace Trust].

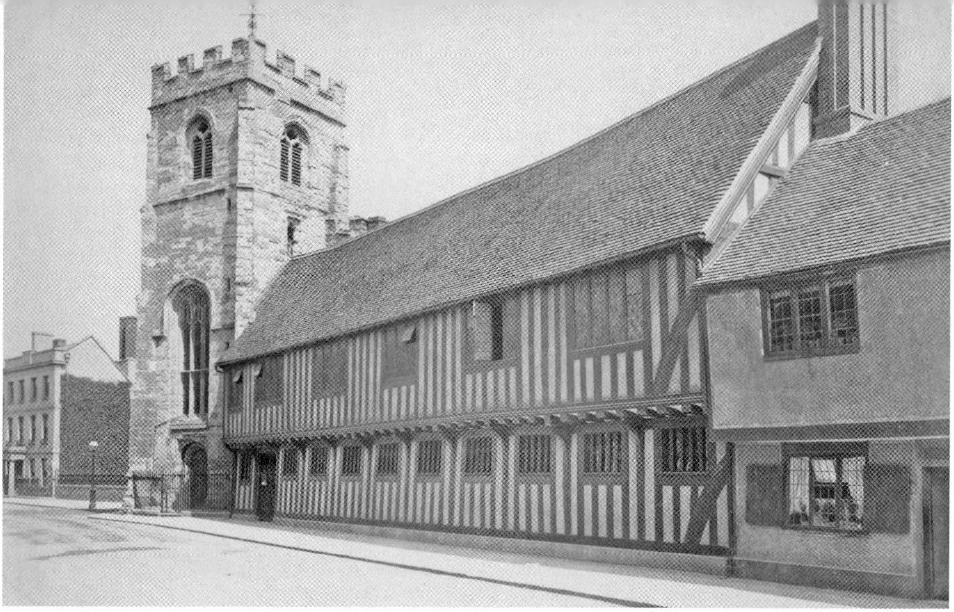

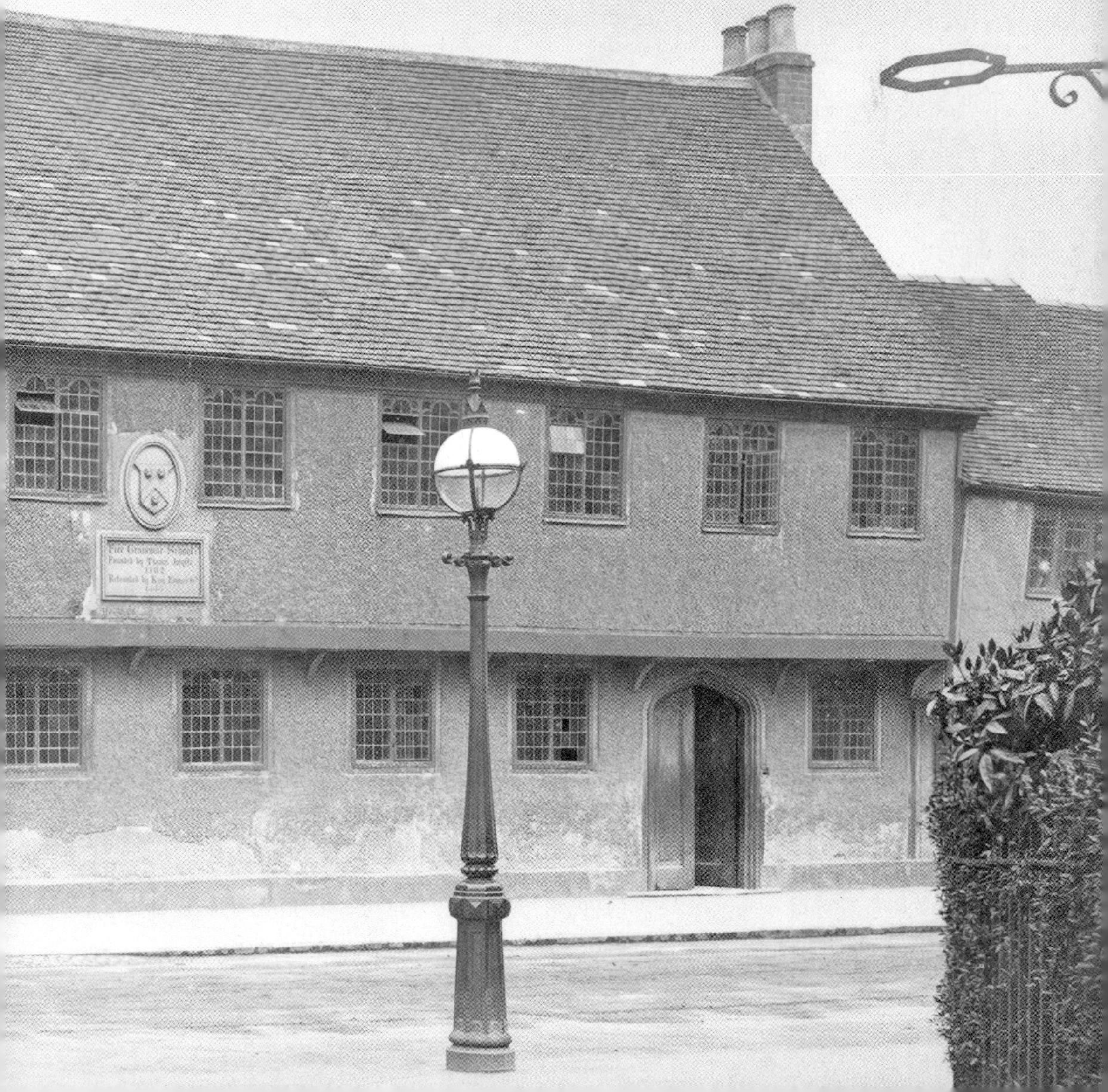

An 1883 print shows the Latin Room at the north end of Big School with the doorway leading to the Mathematics Room.

> "The increasing number of visitors who desire to view the buildings of Shakespeare's School has rendered it necessary to close the School to all visitors except between the hours of 12.30 and 2, and 4.30 and 6pm. A custodian has been appointed, and during these hours occupies the porter's lodge. The charge for admittance has been fixed at threepence. So far the innovation has proved a great success, and a large number of visitors pass through the class-rooms every week."

The office of Head Boy was created in 1892 and Ralph was its first holder, not just for one year but for two. Another Laffan initiative, this one from the Headmaster's wife, was the Shakespeare Birthday procession. What started out on 23rd April 1893 as a modest affair with a muster of all the boys of the school in the Guildhall who then walked in procession to Holy Trinity Church where a wreath was placed on Shakespeare's grave, has since grown into an international gathering, the biggest annual event in the town's calendar. Ralph as Senior Boy was at the head of the inaugural procession and later wrote about it (*"a happy ceremony"*) in *The Stratfordian*. A fuller account of the event appeared in the *Stratford-upon-Avon Herald* under the title *Floral Tributes*:

> "The scholars of the Grammar School did not allow the anniversary of the birth and death of their greatest schoolfellow to pass without paying a tribute to his immortal memory. On Saturday evening a number of them assembled at the Guild Hall, and, in company with the head-master (the Rev. R.S.de C. Laffan) and his assistants, walked to the church for the purpose of placing a wreath on Shakespeare's tomb. In the chancel they were received by the Vicar, addressing

The Latin Room looking northwards circa 1892. [By kind permission of the Shakespeare Birthplace Trust].

> whom Mr. Laffan said that as members of Shakespeare's school they had come to ask him, as custodian of the tomb, to accept the wreath which they offered as a token of their reverence for their great schoolfellow, and to offer their thanks to Almighty God for the great gift which in Shakespeare he had given to Stratford, and through Stratford to England and the world. …The wreath was then deposited on the tomb, the inscription accompanying it being – 'To the memory of William Shakespeare, from the members of Shakespeare's school'."

Although the evidence is lacking, it is highly likely that Ralph was active in other spheres of school life. Music and Debating Societies had been formed during Laffan's tenure and given his pedigree as member of a musically-absorbed family, and given also his later heavy involvement with the Debating Society while at Pembroke College, it is highly likely that Ralph was involved with both while at K.E.S.

Chapter 4

King Edward VI School: (III) The Scholar

In the latter half of the nineteenth century the K.E.S. curriculum was, as in all the endowed grammar schools, stuck in an academic backwater with Latin continuing to prevail in a narrow range of subjects. However, while a broadening of the curriculum was all-too-slowly getting under way (the teaching of French was introduced at K.E.S. in 1868, for example) it was Laffan in the late 1880s and early 1890s who had both the insight and zeal to remodel the curriculum better to meet the needs of those on whose custom the school depended, while at the same time strengthening the provision of the core subject (Latin). The most significant of his changes was the introduction of "Modern" subjects. These included Science (Laffan opened a small laboratory), Modern Languages (German now joining French), and Commercial subjects. The School Prospectus of 1888 states that it *"prepares boys either for the Universities, or for the Military and I.C.S. (Indian Civil Service) Examinations, or for business life."* Boys aiming for the first three of the above were guaranteed instruction by masters who were graduates of Oxford or Cambridge (or Paris in the case of French) *"in the highest honours."* Advanced Mathematics was introduced and was of special interest to boys who wished to work for the Sandhurst examination. For boys *"intended for business life"* a commercial class was formed, offering Book-keeping and Shorthand. Drawing (*"Freehand and Geometrical"*) was available and a carpenters' shop opened.

Laffan's buttressing of the teaching side of K.E.S. (additional staff, new subjects et al), combined with his own natural ability, meant that Ralph prospered in his studies. The evidence for this is to be found in the reports of

4. King Edward VI School: (III) The Scholar

the external examiners, in the published notices of school prizes that were awarded, and in the presentation copies of the several handsomely bound books awarded to Ralph now held in the school Archive.

The examiners from Oxford University visited each year towards the end of the summer term and spent three or four days in the school, reporting to the Governors on its work and discipline. Their report was a vital document as it was published and circulated locally, making it a most important form of publicity for the school. Presentation of their findings was, in the early days, fairly "broad brush" with the performance of each class (i.e. year group) rated for each subject and only the high achievers identified by name. Ralph is first mentioned in the Examiner's Report of 1886 where in Latin he is described as *"conspicuous in the Lower School"* and is awarded the first of his many volumes with a prize book-plate on the front paste-down (see below). In the following year his class (Form III) was commended as *"a promising form which deserves much praise."* In Form IV he is brought into focus when he is identified as *"one of two boys who distinguished themselves"* by gaining 92% in Algebra (*"excellent"*).

It was in the Vth Form (1889-90), however, that Ralph really began to make his mark. In Divinity he *"did specially good work"*; in Latin his Virgil translation *"was particularly good"*; in Greek *"he knew his Greek play well"*; and in German his *"all-round excellence"* was noted. At the Annual Prize Giving held in October 1890 he won all the Form V subject prizes except that for Latin. The reason for this omission may have been due to his candidature that year for the Junior Oxford Local Examination, for which he was awarded Distinction in Latin. He surpassed this accomplishment the following year when, still only fifteen years old and still a junior, he was entered for the Senior Examination (for candidates up to nineteen years) and passed in Divinity, Latin, Mathematics and

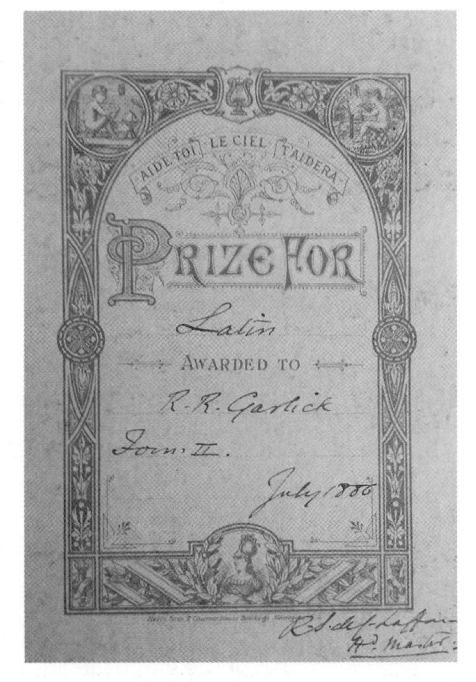

The Form II Prize for Latin was the first of many.

French, an achievement which conferred on him the degree of Associate of Arts at the University of Oxford. His Distinction in Latin meant that he was *"one of the two youngest boys in all England who attained this honour."* (Headmaster's Report 1891).

Ralph continued to earn plaudits in the VIth Form. In the summer of 1892 he obtained the highest marks in both the Latin papers set by the Examiner and was awarded *"the special prize"* for his translation of a Latin poem. The highest marks were also earned in both Greek and Latin papers, while in Higher Mathematics he *"acquitted himself creditably."* Now sixteen, he built on the previous year's success in the Senior Oxford Local Examination by adding Distinction in Greek to that in Latin, giving him a standing of 13th in the Distinction List for the former and 14th for the latter.

There was no let up during the following year – notwithstanding the disruption to studies caused by the ongoing restoration work discussed

Prize Giving 1892.

A part of Ralph's collection of K.E.S. prizes.

previously. Consistently high marks were scored in Latin (low 90s/high 80s across all papers) and Higher Mathematics (*"did well across all papers, obtaining full marks in one"*). There was one anomaly: an 80% scored in Shorthand, a subject he would have followed in the recently-created Commercial Class, but which would have provided him with a skill which doubtless would go on to serve him well in his chosen profession.

The academic year 1892/93 culminated for Ralph with the award of the Delawarr Scholarship and the announcement by the Headmaster that he *"at the early age of seventeen, and against competitors many of them very much older than himself, had won the 1st Open Classical Exhibition at Wadham College (Oxford)."* Wadham, however, was not to be his destination. He resigned the Exhibition in February 1894 in favour of the 1st Open Classical Scholarship at Pembroke College, Oxford, the announcement of which was carried in 24th March 1894 issues of both the *Oxford Journal* and the *Leamington Spa Courier*. This was a prestigious award, the other Open Scholarships at Pembroke that year were

Two prize bound books carrying the K.E.S. crest.

won by candidates from Winchester and Marlborough Colleges. The Editorial of the 1894 issue of *The Stratfordian* stated that:

> *"Great enthusiasm greeted the news of the head of school's success, both Garlick and Mr. Richards (staff) receiving the congratulations of the assembled school. The Headmaster gave a whole holiday in honour of the occasion."*

Predictably, the end of year Examiner, already well acquainted with Ralph from his previous visit, reported that *"Garlick has since last year distinguished himself, as I anticipated he would,"* before going on to commend him for his Latin, French, English History, and General Paper.

The Council Chamber circa 1898. The oak table which carries Ralph's signature is at the bottom of the picture. The open door to the right leads to "Shakespeare's Schoolroom".

4. King Edward VI School: (III) The Scholar

The early seventeenth century oak table in the Council Chamber on which Ralph has carved his initials (R G).

When Ralph finally took leave of the School in August 1894 he did so not only amidst popular acclaim but also with a trove of prizes. However, he did not do so without leaving his mark – literally! It had already become the custom for senior boys to carve their names or initials on the seventeenth century oak table in the Council Chamber and Ralph's can be clearly seen alongside those of some of his contemporaries.

Ralph returned to K.E.S. a few months later for the Annual Prize Giving – but this time as a guest (*"Mr R.R. Garlick (Pembroke College)"*), allowing him to add a further three presentation volumes to his burgeoning library.

It appears, however, to have been a case of one Garlick out, one Garlick in. In the 1896 edition of *Kelly's Directory* the entry for King Edward VI School lists a *"G. Garlick"* as an assistant master. Ralph's father George, it will be remembered, had been teaching music in schools and privately in the town since the early 1860s and therefore his appointment to the staff of the grammar school as (presumably) a music teacher is not unexpected.

29

Chapter 5

Pembroke College, Oxford

In heading for Oxford, Ralph was following a well-trodden path for academics. The traffic, however, had been largely inward as virtually all of the grammar school's headmasters had been Oxford men, including the two responsible for the young William Shakespeare's education, Simon Hunt and Thomas Jenkins. Ralph's own headmaster the Rev. Laffan, of course, was a graduate of Merton College. Doubtless Ralph would also have been aware that Pembroke offered another link (admittedly a somewhat tenuous one) to William Shakespeare in the person of one of its notable alumni, Samuel Johnson (1709-1775), essayist, literary critic and author of the first English dictionary. His *Dictionary of the English Language* was published in 1755 and brought him fame (but not fortune) and endowed him with the nick-name *"Dictionary Johnson"*. Johnson had been interested in Shakespeare all his life. He told his biographer James Boswell (1740-1795) that *"he read Shakespeare at a period so early, that the speech of the Ghost in Hamlet terrified him when he was alone."*[8] A foremost task for Johnson in the preparation of the Dictionary had been the collecting and sorting of thousands of quotations from Shakespeare's plays and this has led a modern Johnsonian scholar to state that these quotations *"made Johnson the unproclaimed but greatest living authority on Shakespeare's diction."*[9] Johnson's interest in Shakespearean scholarship resumed after publication of the Dictionary and he engaged in the task of producing his own edition of Shakespeare's collected works, which belatedly appeared, with an acclaimed Preface, in 1765.

Johnson, although a Shakespeare scholar, never visited Stratford. Nevertheless he did have a connection with the town, as Ralph would have known. The link lay through Johnson's friend (and former pupil) the actor

1875 photo of the Old Quad showing the entrance tower. Ralph occupied a top floor room in "Staircase 6" which is to the left of the archway on the far left of the picture. He paid a termly rent of £3.10s.

Samuel Johnson's rooms can be seen above the doorway (centre left) on the second floor.

David Garrick who organized a Shakespeare Jubilee in Stratford over three days in September 1769. It was the first major commemoration of Shakespeare anywhere in the world. Boswell thought it a shame that Johnson did not join the celebrations: *"almost every man of eminence in the literary world was happy to partake in this festival of genius, (and) the absence of Johnson could not but be wondered at and regretted."*

Johnson studied at Pembroke from October 1728 to December 1729 (when the money from the inheritance upon which he depended ran out) and had rooms in the Lodge Tower which overlooked the quadrangle. Boswell later wrote that Johnson *"contracted a love and regard for Pembroke College, which he retained to the last"* and he bequeathed to the College copies of his works.

That Ralph chose to join the College's *Johnson Society* will occasion no surprise. At each of the Society's monthly meetings a member would present a paper on a literary subject, which would then be followed by a discussion. The meeting was held in the room of the member giving the presentation and in May 1896 Ralph was the appointed host. Understandably, for his maiden presentation he chose a subject on which he could speak with some authority: *"The Influence of Stratford-on-Avon upon Shakespeare."* The Society's Log Book records, somewhat floridly:

"The paper proved exceptionally interesting and admirable since the subject enabled the hon. member to impart to it the picturesqueness and vitality engendered only by personal knowledge in addition to that felicitous expression of imaginative colouring which would in any case be forthcoming. The influences derived from lineage, from early education and companionship, and above all from the Arcadian features of the locality, were set forth and illustrated with a graphic touch. The paper was enlivened by variety. Appreciation of landscape, glimpses of folk-lore, miniatures of fancy and vignettes of fact, made up a charming whole, manifold but not diffusive: while illustrative selections from Shakespeare himself, and an apposite quotation from the Italian, kept the literary aspect of the subject well in view."

The report concludes that *"an eager discussion ensued"* which lasted *"until Morpheus claimed his own."*[10]

Ralph's next foray with the *Johnson Society* occurred at the end of the following term when he read a Paper on *Madame de Stael* (1766-1817), the French woman of letters, political propagandist and conversationalist. In the following Lent term (1897) he was elected Hon. Secretary of the Society and later presented his final Paper on *Edmund Burke* (1729-1797), the Irish-born highly influential politician and political thinker who was notable for his strong support for the American Revolution and his fierce opposition to the French Revolution. Burke was also a founder member of Johnson's *Literary Club*, a dining fraternity formed in 1764 with nine members whose principal function was to allow its members to eat, drink and debate informally.

It has been conjectured (in the absence of records) that Ralph had been a member of the Debating Society while at K.E.S. but at Pembroke he was most certainly a debater. During his first term his contributions were exclusively from the floor but in February 1895 he proposed the motion: *"In the opinion of this House the establishment of a complete democracy in England would be a death-blow to England's greatness."* (He may not have been too disappointed that the motion was lost!). At the start of his second academic year (1895) he joined the Committee and continued to be involved in its debates, both from the floor and from the lectern.

The third society to which Ralph belonged at Pembroke was the *Beaumont*, named for Francis Beaumont (1584-1616), Elizabethan dramatist and best-known for his collaborations with John Fletcher (1579-1625); together they were the most important playwrights of the generation following Shakespeare. Ralph was one of twelve Pembrokians who, in March of his second year, formed the Society, its stated object being *"the Reading and Discussion of Papers on Literary subjects."* Its membership was to be fairly exclusive, Rule IV of its constitution stating: *"That the Numbers of this Society be limited to Twelve."* The anticipated longevity of the Society was implied in Rule XII which declared: *"That all members who have gone down…and who have taken their degrees, be called Life Members."* At the Society's second meeting members *"chose a Ribbon and a Tie to be worn by members."* Later that year Ralph read a Paper on *The Ossianic Poems*[11] and *"a discussion ensued on the interesting pieces of verse which formed the subject of the poem."* Unfortunately the Society was not destined to endure, its survival presumably not helped by its exclusiveness (Rule IV).

Cerebral interests were not the only ones to occupy Ralph at Pembroke. Despite growing up but a short distance from the headquarters of the Town's Boat Club on the River Avon (founded 1874) Ralph had not been an oarsman,[12] but it was a sport he took up at Oxford with some success. The fundamentals of rowing were learned in "Tubbing"[13] before he and the other novice freshmen graduated to the "Robinson Fours" which comprised four boats of four oarsmen each coached by an experienced member of the College Eight. Ralph's progress was such that he was selected for the College Eight for "Torpids", a series of bumping races held in the Hilary (Lent) term. To the frustration of the oarsmen from all the Oxford colleges the 1895 Torpids had to be cancelled because of the icy conditions. However, the several inter-collegiate races went ahead as scheduled in the summer term with Ralph now fully integrated into the Pembroke Eight.

By the beginning of his second year Ralph was a sufficiently experienced oarsman to be appointed coach to one of the "Robinson Fours". Although he did not row in the 1896 Torpids he did feature at stroke (weighing 11 stone 4 pounds) for the Summer Eights. He also rowed in Fours and Pairs that year, but appears not to have sculled. By the start of his third year he was considered a "senior" and was elected to the Pembroke Boat Club Committee. He featured in the 1897 Torpids (at last!) and had a full summer of rowing in Eights, Fours and Pairs. His progress was such that he was appointed Captain of the Boat Club for his final year and was one of three Pembroke men entered for the University's "Trial Eights", though none were selected for the Oxford boat. His rowing programme for the remainder of the year followed the by-now familiar pattern of Eights, Fours and Pairs.

Left: Pembroke College Eight circa 1898. Ralph is seated, second right.
Right: Ralph's Eight in action.

5. Pembroke College, Oxford

His final outing for the College, however, did not come, as would be expected, in his last summer before coming down. It came instead in the following summer of 1899 when, it would appear, the Club were short of an oarsman and Ralph stepped in at no. 6. The Boat Club records report that:

> "Mr R.R. Garlick, Boatcaptain of the previous year, had patriotically come up, at some personal inconvenience, to row in the boat."

Although Ralph had moved into a more rarefied milieu when he went up to Oxford he did not forget his old School. (He would, of course, have received a visual reminder of it every time he returned home on vacation.) He played cricket for the K.E.S. (Past) in a match against K.E.S. (Present) on the school ground in July 1895. While he does not appear to have continued playing rugby while at Pembroke, he was fit and willing enough to turn out for the Old Boys side of November 1898 which defeated the School 1st XV by *"two goals and four tries to one goal and one try."*

His contact with the School was also maintained via the printed word. In the December 1895 issue of *The Stratfordian*, under the heading *"Oxford Letter"* Ralph mused on the various goings-on at the University, from the trivial (at Trinity College *"a squib exploded in a certain room and, setting fire to the curtains, burnt it down"*) to the utilitarian (Mr Atkinson of St. John's College had invented an instrument for rowers which *"is fixed on the rowlocks of the boat and records the amount of work done by each oar each minute"*). He was sanguine about the College Eight's prospects but far less so about the University's football (*"below average"*) and rugby where some *"alterations must be made in our front line"* if the Oxford forwards are not to be *"run over by the Cambridge pack."* On the

Ralph won a number of trophies for rowing at Pembroke.

political front he notes *"the ever-growing Socialist element in Oxford"* which was manifested in William Morris's public lecture on *"The Future of Socialism."*

In a second *"Oxford Letter"* published in the October 1896 issue he again discourses on Torpids, "Socker" and "Rugger football" but is also moved to write about *"the all-absorbing topic of Women's Degrees."* Although ladies were by then being admitted to the University (*"a concession,"* wrote Ralph, *"somewhat ungraciously granted by the jealous male"*) a motion to allow them to be awarded a degree at the end of their course of study *"was thrown out in Convocation."* By aligning himself with *"some of the most enlightened of Oxford Dons"* who supported the motion, Ralph was revealing his liberal credentials.

While the award of a 3rd Class BA in Litterae Humaniores (Greats) in October 1898 marked the end of Ralph's undergraduate days at Pembroke, his involvement with the University appears to have continued into the following year as noted – at Pembroke with his emergency recall to the College Eight in the summer of 1899 – and at an unspecified college for Indian studies during his Indian Civil Service probationary year.

College photograph taken in summer 1898. Ralph is on the back row, 6th from left, his arm held across his chest.

Part 2

INDIA

" 'Twas for the good of my country that I should be abroad"

George Farquhar, The Beaux, Stratagem, 1707

Chapter 6

The Steel Frame of India

"It was a bold idea to let loose on India, with her ancient civilisations and differing religions, cultures and languages, a succession of brash young men newly emerged from the academic disciplines in which British universities had trained them, and give them enormous responsibilities in the most attractive career conceivable. So I joined the Indian Civil Service."[14]

The Jewel In The Crown

The British Raj in 1900 comprised India, Pakistan, Bangladesh and Burma with a population of more than 300 million people. Britain held India for its great economic, strategic and military value.

India lay at the heart of Britain's maritime network, lying as she did astride the great commercial shipping routes linking her to the Far East. She was also a vital staging post on voyages both to and from Britain's dominions of Australia and New Zealand.

India's military significance grew during the second half of the nineteenth century. Indian troops were deployed not only to protect British interests in India itself and for the defence of its frontiers, but also to safeguard its trade-routes and to secure its imperial interests in China, Africa, and the Middle East. Indian soldiers were also, in the next century, to play a significant role in both World Wars.

Above all India played a vital economic role in sustaining Britain's position as a world power. She exported to Britain a variety of raw materials and foodstuffs – cotton, rice, jute, wool, rubber, tea and wheat. Just as significant, if not a little more so, was India's value as a market for British exports; indeed she was Britain's largest single export market. In 1913 Britain supplied over 60 per cent of India's imports, Britain's staple industries being the main beneficiaries – cotton, iron, steel and engineering, and chemicals. Britain also sustained important investment links with the subcontinent. In the late nineteenth century nearly one-fifth of Britain's overseas investment was in India, a major part in government loans but also in infrastructure (especially railway construction), and in tea and coffee plantations.

India held a singular and idealistic place in the British imagination, especially so after 1876 when Queen Victoria was made Empress of India. The phrase "jewel in the crown" was coined from a speech given by Benjamin Disraeli in 1872 and came to reference India's prestige and glamour. (*"The Jewel in the Crown"* was the title of a highly-acclaimed 1984 television series in which one of the leading parts was played by Tim Pigott-Smith, another Old Boy of K.E.S.) Lord Curzon, the last Victorian Viceroy of India, had a pithy take on India's value to Britain when he wrote: *"While we hold onto India, we are a first-rate power. If we lose India, we will decline to a third-rate power."*[15]

It was the East India Company (EIC), an English (later British) joint-stock company which first gained a foothold in India, going on to expand and conquer until by the end of the eighteenth century the Company had gained control of virtually all India, although regulated as a subsidiary of the Crown. The Indian Rebellion of 1857/58 led to the Company's abolition by Parliament and from 1858 India was ruled by the Crown, its representative in India being the Viceroy. Although they reported to the Secretary of State for India (a political appointment), the Viceroys were largely free to exercise their authority over an entire subcontinent, which made them among the most powerful men on earth in the Victorian and Edwardian eras. They had at their disposal two all-powerful agencies: the British Indian Army and the Indian Civil Service (ICS).

The Indian Civil Service

It was the ICS which provided India with its administrators, magistrates and judges and was the organization that Ralph aspired to join when he had obtained his degree. He would have been unable to do so some forty years earlier as selection for the Indian civil service under the East India Company was by patronage; all candidates for Haileybury, the college where all civil servants of the EIC were trained, had to be nominated by the Company's

6. The Steel Frame of India

directors. By 1855, however, the British Government had opened recruitment to competition, thereby ensuring selection by merit rather than by patronage. Candidates for admission to the ICS were now required to sit a competitive examination which was held at Burlington House in London once a year. Ralph would have (very nearly) fitted the typical profile of such a candidate.

For most of the applicants the crucial years of their education would have been spent at a public school. (Cheltenham College was the leading supplier of entrants, while Marlborough and Rugby followed some way behind). An English public school background, with its emphasis on the teaching of classics and history, its powerful games ethos, and its strict adherence to ideas of truth, honesty, fair play and decency, was believed to equip its products with the virtues regarded as indispensable for running the Empire. In their early twenties young men were charged with authority over thousands of Indian lives. However, following the introduction of open competition in the search for talent, the chances for those with a grammar school education had improved markedly. It could be argued, with some substance, that the grammar schools matched the strengths of the public school while avoiding its weaknesses.

While Ralph's grammar school background, combined with an Oxford Classics degree, made him an ideal candidate for the examinations set by the Commissioners of the ICS, the question of motive arises. Why might a twenty-two year old, whose experiences of life hitherto had been largely confined to Stratford and Oxford, have contemplated a life in exile on the Indian subcontinent? For one retired senior ICS officer the Service was the perfect choice. Speaking to potential undergraduate recruits in 1903 he was unconstrained in his praise:

"I venture to recommend it, not merely because, on the whole, it pays much better than most professions, but because it offers an able and ambitious young man an honourable and manly career, giving him full scope for exercise of the strongest character and the highest intellectual power, and holding out promise of eminent distinction. The most valuable prizes and the most honourable distinctions of the Service are freely open to all qualified competitors."[16]

Two possible influences on Ralph can be discounted. Firstly, kinship will have played no part as he had no connection with India. (Some members of the ICS had their careers decided for them by long-standing family links.) Secondly, a number of candidates will have been influenced by the growth of imperialist sentiment in Britain in the 1880s and '90s. Such men will have entertained a vision of an active outdoor life, governing the native people with vigour and benevolence.

In contrast, given his temperament, his likely political leanings, and his strongly-held Christian faith, Ralph's motives are likely to have been of an altruistic nature, holding to the belief that he was following a vocation and not just seeking a career. This sense of mission was the sentiment of the Victorian civil servant who wrote of *"the joy of feeling that one is working and ruling and making oneself useful in God's world."*

Another credible influence takes us back to K.E.S. and Ralph's old headmaster. Young men sometimes went into the ICS because they were encouraged by a schoolmaster and this might have been the case with Ralph for, after leaving Winchester but before entering Merton College in 1874, the Rev. Laffan had spent three years in the ICS. He might, at the very least, have planted the germ of an idea in any discussion concerning Ralph's career planning. Furthermore, Ralph would not have been the first K.E.S. pupil that he had recommended for the ICS. Herbert Samman, who was five years ahead of Ralph at K.E.S., took fifth place in the Open Examination for the ICS in 1890, prompting Laffan to write: *"We have every cause to be proud of this result."*

Above all, there was the prestige and the financial rewards to be had from attachment to the ICS. It was said that no other position in the British Empire enjoyed greater prestige and the emoluments and pensions were handsome. While the pay of a Civilian (the nomenclature of members of the ICS) at the start of his career was *"ordinarily very moderate,"* it became progressively more generous with seniority and advancement. A Civilian could expect to earn significantly more than he could hope to earn at home, was entitled to generous allowances, and enjoyed astonishing security of tenure. Living in India also offered him the chance to live in a life-style that he could never have afforded at home. Pensions were generous. After twenty-five years of service in India an officer, irrespective of position, was eligible for a pension of £1,000 a year. Provision was also made for the family. The widow of an officer of more than twelve years' service, or the widow of a senior officer, was entitled to £300 a year. The allowances for children ranged from £25 to £100 according to age and ceased, in the case of a boy, at the age of 21, and, in the case of a girl, on marriage. A daughter also received £250 as a marriage portion. For Ralph's immediate family these pension arrangements would turn out to be of singular importance.

6. The Steel Frame of India

Any of the above, or a combination of all three, might have induced Ralph to try for the ICS. In the summer of 1899 he would have been one of some two hundred candidates competing for about forty places who sat the Civil Service Examination at Burlington House in Piccadilly. He was successful at this first hurdle, passing 57th. After hearing the result he would have returned to London for a medical examination and to choose his Indian province. His choice was not unfettered, however, but was determined by the position he had obtained in the examination. Had he finished in the top rank he is likely to have chosen the Punjab or the United Provinces. However, he did moderately well and was able to opt for Bengal, thus avoiding the less-favoured Madras and the least-favoured Burma. The advantages of Bengal, a vast province of over 70 million people, were that it contained Calcutta, the imperial capital and administrative centre, and therefore offered good prospects for advancement. Its drawbacks were its lack of cities, difficulties of travel, and its unrelenting humidity. It also came to be associated, increasingly so as the twentieth century unfolded, with violent nationalism.

Having successfully negotiated the first couple of hurdles (examination and medical) another lay ahead. In India the duties of Civilians required them to make journeys on horseback and therefore they were expected to be

All examinations for entry to the ICS were held at Burlington House in Piccadilly.

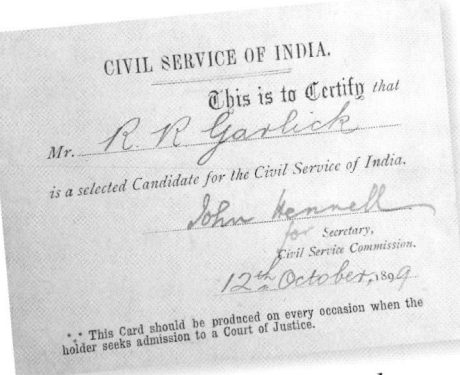

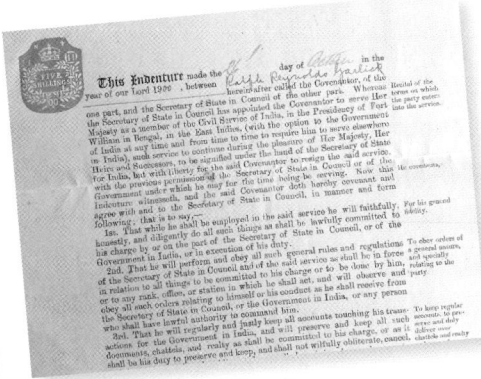

Ralph's Admission Card.

Ralph's Indenture.

Ralph's Appointment to Bengal.

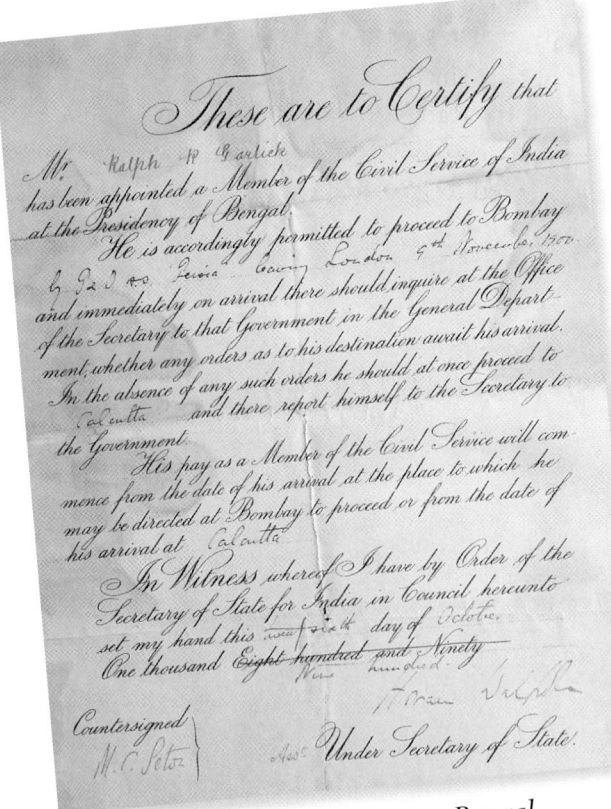

Ralph's Covenant.

reasonably proficient in riding. As he was not from a *"hunting, shooting, fishing"* background Ralph would have had to find a riding school which would have brought him up to the required standard of horsemanship.

The successful candidates would spend the next year as probationers at an approved university. During this training they received £300 a year, which for many (like Ralph) who had scraped through a degree course on much less, was a princely sum. Oxford had acquired a well-founded reputation for its training of civil servants for India, the probationers being enrolled in several of its Colleges which jointly appointed teachers for them. The curriculum was largely academic, however. The probationers studied the laws and institutions of India, learned a classical language (Sanskrit, Arabic or Persian), studied Indian history and geography, and learned the chief vernacular of the Province to which they had been assigned – although this would be of doubtful value when a variety of languages is likely to have been spoken. Their only practical knowledge came by way of sittings at the Old Bailey and at the Marylebone and Bow Street Courts where they were introduced to the law.

Such were the commitments that Ralph would have been required to undertake during his probationary year of 1898-1899. Unfortunately there is no conclusive evidence that he returned to Oxford for the duration (his name does not appear in the main University records for the period in question) but circumstantial evidence suggests that he did so. While his name was removed from the books of Pembroke College on his graduation in October 1898 it reappeared in 1899, though no reason is specified. Possibly linked to this event is the knowledge that he rowed in the College Eights of that year (page 34). It is unreasonable to think that he would have undertaken his probationary year at any university other than his own.

His probationary year completed, Ralph sat the ICS Final Examination at Burlington House in the summer of 1900 and passed 39th. With all the hurdles now overcome it remained only for him to attend the India Office in order to sign his covenant (contract), by which he agreed to observe all Government regulations. He was now primed for a life in the Service.

Passage To India

Preparatory to embarking on his first overseas posting, and recognizing that he would not have been due his first home leave until he had been about four or five years in India, Ralph would have had a great many preparations to undertake.

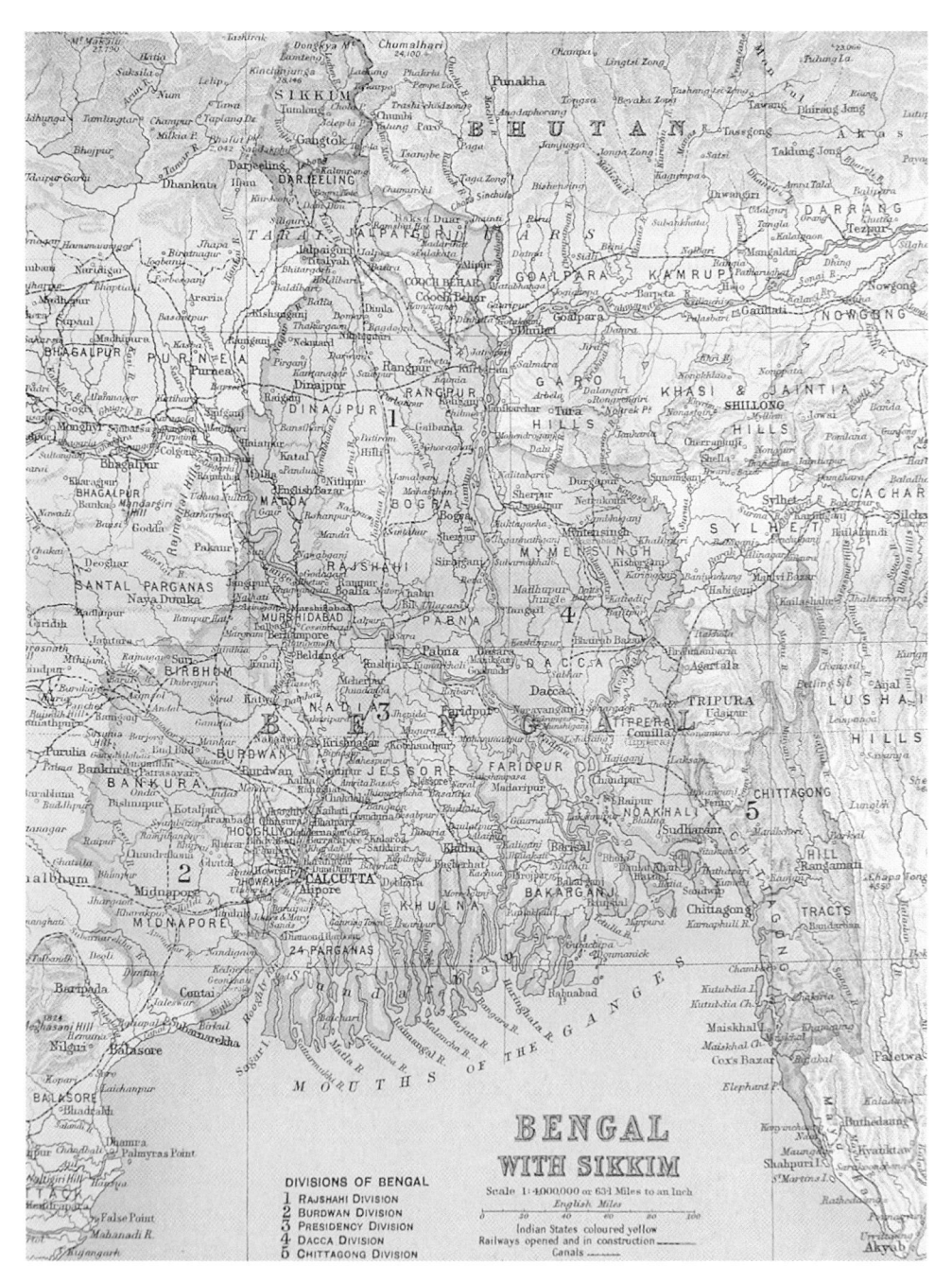

Map of Bengal, Ex Imperial Gazetteer, India. Published by John Bartholomew 1931. Alipore is directly below Calcutta.

6. The Steel Frame of India

Old "India hands" will have been an invaluable source of advice, with regard to kit and clothing in particular. He would have required a fairly formidable wardrobe, necessitated by variations in both seasonal weather (hot and cold, wet and dry) and the requirements of protocol (formal/informal attire). He would also have done his best to learn as much as he could about his designated province, Bengal – its mix of races, religions, customs and languages. It would have been surprising if he had not also read at least some of the works of Rudyard Kipling, the principal chronicler of British India.[17] Along with his kit and wardrobe he would have packed two items of essential reading for griffins (the term used to describe ICS officers in their first year): the *ICS Handbook* and the ICS booklet *"Hints for Young Civilians"*.

Voyages to India had once taken several months by sail via the Cape of Good Hope. Since the opening of the Suez Canal in 1869 and the advent of steam, the journey could now be undertaken in around three weeks. Ralph embarked at Tilbury on 7th November 1900, a popular time of year for India-bound passengers because it brought them out at the beginning of the Cold Weather – and it was also in time for Christmas. His vessel was the 4,200 ton *"Persia"* belonging to the Peninsular and Oriental Navigation Company (P&O). P&O was known as the Exile's Line and was always reckoned to be

Ralph travelled from Liverpool to Calcutta on S.S. City of Nagpur in October 1926.

the smartest. This was to be the first of a number of passages in both directions taken by Ralph (and/or his family) over the next thirty years. This first three weeks plus passage to India will have given Ralph time, by gradual degree, to decouple himself from the familiar sights and sounds of home and to prepare for the land of extremes to which he was bound – extremes of climate and of wealth, in particular.

From the Thames the *"Persia"* sailed down the Channel and crossed the Bay of Biscay before entering the Mediterranean and heading eastwards. Various stops will have been made before reaching Port Said, roughly the half-way point. Here a pilot was taken on board before the vessel proceeded slowly (6 mph) down the Canal. Aden (for coaling) was the last port of call before the final run across the Indian Ocean to Bombay which was reached on 3rd December. Here Ralph will have been met, assisted through customs with his baggage, and taken to his accommodation before being readied for the last stage of his journey – the 1,421 miles by train (First Class) to Calcutta. On arrival he would have been greeted, briefed and given details of the district and sub-district to which he had been posted.

The district, of which there were some 250 at the time of Ralph's arrival in India, was British India's key administrative unit. At its head was the District Officer (or "D.O.")[18], often referred to as the *"backbone of the*

Ralph's much-travelled trunk.

The trunk's luggage label. P&O was always reckoned to be the smartest of the steamship lines.

6. The Steel Frame of India

administration". Each was in charge of an area which averaged 4,500 square miles (the average size of an English county is about 1,000 square miles). Each was responsible for the welfare of a population which averaged about a million, but a population that was extraordinarily diverse. It included jungle dwellers and urban townsmen, wealthy landowners and tenant farmers, illiterate villagers and highly-educated city dwellers, with religious and language differences adding to the mix. Each district was divided into four or five sub-divisions which were in the charge of sub-divisional officers who were, in effect, the D.O.'s lieutenants.

The District Officer had multiple responsibilities, the collection of land and other revenues (hence the title of Collector) being among the more important. As chief magistrate of the district he handled few cases of his own but dealt rather with appeals from his several assistant magistrates and supervised the work of all magisterial courts. Above all he was responsible for the prevention and suppression of crime and the preservation of peace, the most serious threats coming from dacoits (gangs of not less than five who robbed with violence) and communal riots. The District Officer's broad remit meant that in the autumn with the arrival of cooler weather he would tour his district not only to see at first-hand what was going on, but also in his role as Collector to inspect and assess for revenue many of the villages that lay within his jurisdiction. Above all, the D.O. was not merely the chief representative of the Government in the district but its personification. In the words of one ex-ICS officer:

> *"His presence was rather like the visit of a medieval sovereign, providing occasion for ordinary people to see what the Raj was about, and to speak in person to its manifestation."*

The headquarters of the district to which Ralph had been appointed would have been reached initially by train, but then onwards by horse or bullock cart to a more remote post. Here he would have been taken under the wing of, and trained by, his first District Officer. He would have provided himself with a bearer who looked after his clothes and ruled the household. If he was living in a place where electricity was not available he also needed servants to pull his fans (*"punkhas"*), known as punkha-wallahs.

Little of what Ralph had learned during the course of his studies at home would have been of a great deal of help now that he was in the field. He would,

An English magistrate administering justice in India (The Graphic 1886).

for example, have studied legal texts but would never have seen the law practised in an Indian court, least of all conducted in a village in the open air. He may have been taught the local language, but would still have found communication with the local population challenging in the extreme.

Ralph would have had to deal with three main requirements during his first year. The first was to learn the local vernacular, of which there might be more than one version. After six months he would have taken the first of a series of examinations, all of which would have included a *viva voce*. The second was to learn the theory of revenue collection which, for practical purposes, would have been combined with excursions into local villages. Thirdly, to learn the law in the field by attending the courts of sub-divisional officers with orders to watch proceedings. The District Officer would also have taken Ralph on tour, not only to familiarize him with the geography of his territory but also to enable him to better understand the people who were to be under his charge.

At the end of six months or so Ralph would have faced his first departmental examination, after which he would have become an assistant magistrate of the third class and his work would have become much more interesting. This would have enabled him to try minor cases which allowed for penalties of up to one month's imprisonment, or more than a trivial fine. By the end of his first year he would have become an assistant magistrate of the second class and begun to try both civil and criminal cases with the power to sentence up to a month's hard labour and to fine up to fifty rupees. Over the next few years he would have taken further departmental examinations and become a *"full-powered"* or *"first-class"* magistrate. Now, at the age of around twenty-five, he would have exercised extensive powers, enabling him, sitting by himself, to try all except the most serious offences. He could sentence an offender to two years' hard labour and a fine of a thousand rupees.

Before Ralph reached this milestone in his career, however, his domestic arrangements had undergone a sea change. On 26th December 1902 he married Daisy Charles in Saint John's Church, Calcutta. It was unusual for a member of the ICS to marry so early in his career (less than two years' service) and so young (Ralph was 25), indeed it was positively discouraged as it made a Civilian poorer (having to support a wife) and less mobile (if encumbered with a family). Most waited until their first home leave when they hoped to return to India with a wife (or to be followed shortly afterwards by a fiancée). Since their first furlough was not due for at least four years many were in their thirties before they married.[19]

Ralph Garlic

Ralph was fortunate to have found his prospective wife in India. Daisy had been born (in 1877) and brought up there, where her father Thomas Charles was Deputy Inspector-General of the Bengal Police. Marriage would not only have enriched his private life but might also have had a bearing on whether to choose a judicial or an administrative future path with the ICS, the latter with the likelihood of distant postings and a peripatetic life-style being ill-suited to family life.

For the first five years of his service Ralph would have remained on a junior grade but he then appears to have been appointed to a superior post when in 1905 he was transferred to the newly-created province of Eastern Bengal and Assam. While Assam had not been a popular posting with ICS officers (frontier life, hostile tribesmen) it would have given Ralph valuable experience in the field and significantly enhanced his promotion prospects. His first independent charge came in 1908 when he was promoted to joint magistrate.

In 1910 Ralph and Daisy returned to England in order to enable Ralph to continue his legal studies. He was admitted as a student to the Inner Temple in London on 6th April. Inner Temple was one of four Inns of Court which provided the training needed by prospective barristers, though in Ralph's

Ralph and Daisy on leave in England circa 1911.

6. The Steel Frame of India

case he was to continue his studies back in India. For the duration of his time at Inner Temple he rented a substantial family house at Lordship Road, Stoke Newington. Originally known as St Mary's Lodge it had been built (and lived in) by a prominent architect of the day, John Young. The 1911 census shows the occupants of the house to have been Ralph and Daisy and their daughter Helena who had been born a couple of months earlier. The household also included two servants and a nurse to look after baby Helena.

In May 1911 Ralph returned to India on his own on the P&O vessel *Himalaya*. The photograph on the next page shows him on the quayside at Tilbury prior to boarding. With his bowler hat and pipe he has a jaunty air, perhaps relishing his recently acquired status as a father, or possibly relishing his prospects of further advancement in the judiciary following his period of study at the Inner Temple.

This duly came in April 1912 when he was appointed a District Judge, which corresponded with a county court judge in England. District Courts administered justice at a district level, had jurisdiction over both criminal and civil cases and heard appeals from magisterial courts. Murder cases were usually either the consequence of a blood feud or the result of murder by either intent or impulse. Ralph's initial appointment was at Third Grade but over the following years he progressed to First Grade with corresponding uplifts in his salary.

All the while he was moving closer to the centre of judicial power in Bengal, the Calcutta High Court which had jurisdiction over the whole province of Bengal and was the oldest High Court in India (established 1862). In March 1928 Ralph was appointed to act as a Judge of the Calcutta High Court for a period of six months. Clearly it was a prestigious post but there were also practical benefits. A judge received a generous salary; enjoyed three months holiday a year; worked fixed hours (leaving him more time for leisure); and (unlike a district judge) did not go on circuit.

Ralph's modus operandi in his court in India was, of course, different in key areas from that of a judge sitting in an English court, notably in respect of his responsibilities. Unlike an English court where the judge heard arguments from opposing counsel who had been trained at the bar, in India Ralph will have tried cases without counsel, asking questions himself of witnesses. The absence of a jury would have added to his responsibilities since he had to decide whether or not the accused was guilty. Furthermore, he had wider discretion than an English judge in deciding the appropriate punishment.

Ralph (centre, in bowler hat and smoking a pipe) at Tilbury in May 1911 preparing to board S.S. "Himalaya" for the voyage to Bombay.

6. The Steel Frame of India

At the end of his Calcutta posting, and following a period of leave in the UK, Ralph returned to India in August 1929 on the *"Rawalpindi"* of the P&O line on what would prove to be his last voyage. His appointment as Senior Sessions Judge of Alipore, an area just south of Calcutta, confirmed his advance to the front rank of the Indian judiciary. Calcutta was now the family home, a family which now comprised not only Ralph and Daisy and daughter Helena but also, when home on holiday from their school in England, their two sons, George (born 1913) and John (born 1917).

Both boys had been sent to schools in England and in the one case the link with Stratford was re-established. In September 1923 George was entered as a boarder to Grove House School in Greenhill Street, whose owner and headmaster was Ralph's brother-in-law William Howe. George therefore had the advantage of living with family as well as being just a short distance from the family home in Wood Street (where his uncle Charles continued to trade). He would not have lacked support and company from his kin. In September 1924 both boys joined Cheltenham College where their father's old headmaster at King Edward VI School had once held office (1895-1899), and in January 1925 they were joined in the town by their older sister Helena who joined Cheltenham Ladies' College as a day girl.

Grove House School in Greenhill Street circa 1920. Headmaster William Howe was Ralph's brother-in-law.

Chapter 7

Turbulent Times

When Ralph resolved to apply for the ICS he would have been well aware of the challenges and risks that he would face there. Paramount among these would have been *"the baneful effects of the climate,"* and the mix of debilitating (and in a few cases, potentially lethal) diseases. Temperatures start to rise in early April and by May are not expected to fall below 100°F, with high humidity adding to the discomfort and causing further ailments, such as fever, stomach cramps, skin infections and prickly heat. Smallpox, dysentery, typhoid, malaria and tetanus were ever-present threats, while cholera was potentially the most dangerous of all. It is no surprise that statistics showed the death rate among serving ICS officers to have been significantly higher than it was for their home-based equivalents.

By contrast, personal safety is likely to have been seen by Ralph as far less of an issue, though not one to be totally ignored. The Indian Mutiny (or Uprising) had occurred little more than forty years earlier, following which the Crown took control from the East India Company and put into effect (albeit gradually) many much-needed economic, legal and educational improvements. The late Victorians believed firmly in the righteousness of their rule, seeing it as a noble mission, its benefits to the indigenous population seemingly obvious. The foundation of the Raj looked secure. Voices calling for a share in government and administration were already beginning to be heard, however, from both British liberals and radicals at home and from select segments within Indian society itself.

The first stirrings of Indian nationalism arose in the 1880s with the founding of the Indian National Congress. Its leaders were drawn mostly from among the western-educated and largely high-caste Hindu urban elite,

7. Turbulent Times

however, and their principal aim was to obtain a greater role in governing their own country. It took the partitioning of Bengal into two parts, Bengal and Eastern Bengal and Assam, in 1905 to thrust the issue of self-rule to the fore (the event which, it will be remembered, occasioned Ralph's transfer to Assam). Although justified by the British on grounds of greater administrative efficiency, the partition angered Bengalis and stimulated nationalist sentiments among the politically conscious and disaffected young in particular. Groups of radicals formed which advocated break-away from Britain and to this end there were, between 1906 and 1908, a number of failed attempts to assassinate those in the upper echelons of government in Bengal. In May 1908 an attempt was made to assassinate District Judge Kingsford who, while serving as Chief Magistrate of the Court of Alipore, had sentenced the editors of a radical Bengali nationalist publication to heavy imprisonment for sedition. Kingsford escaped the bomb that was thrown but it killed his two female bridge partners. A number of suspects were arrested and charged with *"organising to wage war against the King"*, setting in motion what came to be known as the *Alipore Bomb Case*. Held in the Alipore Sessions Court, the court which was to be the backcloth for a far more deadly event some two decades later, the hearings generated a great deal of interest in both the British and Indian press and resulted in two death sentences, both commuted to life imprisonment.[20] In the aftermath of the trial the radical nationalists went underground and between 1909 and 1914 continued their campaign with a series of targeted assassinations against Raj officials with variable success.

With the outbreak of war in 1914 any ideas that the Germans might have had that, in a European war, India would be a liability swiftly evaporated in the face of an outpouring of support from all parties. The Indian contribution to the war effort was weighty in both men and resources. About 1.3 million Indian combatants and non-combatants served on all fronts while foodstuffs, munitions and textiles were supplied in quantity. Indian jute, for example, was in heavy demand for the sandbags which lined the trenches and castor oil from Southern India was supplied as the lubricant for rotary aero engines. While some anti-colonial activity continued, particularly in Bengal and Punjab, it was on a much reduced scale. The mainstream leadership believed their country's enormous services to the British Empire during the war would be rewarded with steps towards self-rule.

In 1919, however, two events occurred which dealt severe blows to moves towards peaceful and *"responsible"* government and stoked nationalist passions.

The British Government extended the restrictive wartime powers into the post-war period (inciting a violent reaction) and in April Brigadier-General Dyer ordered Indian army troops to open fire on a predominantly Sikh crowd at Amritsar, killing between 500 and 600 and wounding many more. A rift had been opened and serious moves towards home-rule, both violent and non-violent, were under way.

The non-violent wing of the Indian nationalist movement was assumed, from 1917 onwards, by Mohandas Gandhi (1869-1948) who used techniques of civil disobedience and non-cooperation, the latter involving a boycott of British goods and institutions (legislatures, courts, etc.). His movement enjoyed widespread popular support but governments in London made only limited constitutional concessions. At the other end of the political spectrum were the underground revolutionary groups which believed in armed revolution against the ruling British and since their avowed targets were leading British administrators the lives of ICS officers were at serious risk. Their weapons of choice were the gun and the bomb.

Gandhi at 10 Downing Street.

In December 1928 a 21 year-old police officer was fatally shot by two revolutionaries in Lahore. Both escaped but one, with a new associate, exploded two bombs inside the Central Legislative Assembly in Delhi the following year. A failed attempt was made to assassinate the Calcutta Police Commissioner in August 1930. Charles Tegart was regarded by Bengal revolutionaries as a fierce opponent of Indian nationalism and had already survived several assassination attempts. A bomb was thrown into the car in which he was travelling but Tegart shot his assailant and escaped unhurt. Less fortunate was F.J. Lowman, Inspector General of Police, who, in August 1930, was shot at close range while undergoing treatment in the Medical School Hospital in Dacca.

One high profile assassination was to have repercussions for Ralph. In December 1930 three revolutionaries targeted the Inspector General of Prisons Lieutenant-General Simpson and shot him seven times while he was sitting in his chair in the headquarters of the Bengal Government and Secretariat. A brief

7. Turbulent Times

Fred Ballance   Walter Gibbs   Judge R. Garlick
Fred Winter   Rev R.M. Goodfield

Above: Ralph, on leave in England circa 1925, with members of the Congregational Church, Stratford-upon-Avon. The Rev Goodfield conducted Ralph's Memorial Service six years later. [By kind permission of the Shakespeare Birthplace Trust].

Below: Lieutenant-General Simpson was murdered by Bengal Revolutionaries in the Secretariat in December 1930.

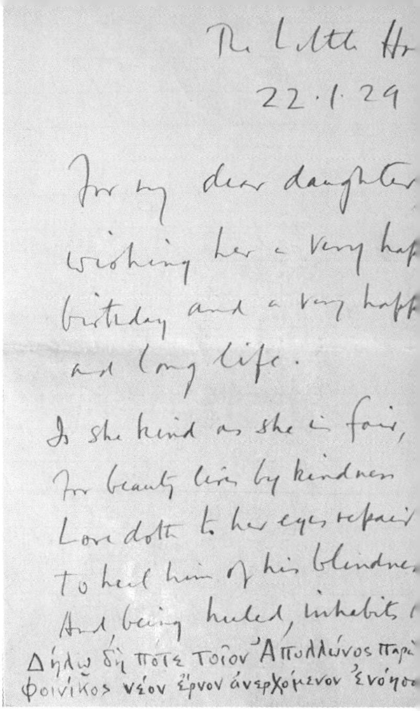

Left: Ralph and Daisy circa 1930. Probably their last photograph. Centre: Ralph and Helena circa 1929. Right: A poetic letter from Ralph to Helena on her eighteenth birthday. He quotes two lines of Greek from the Odyssey: "Once on *[the island of]* Delos by the altar of Apollo I saw such a thing, a young shoot of a palm tree springing up."

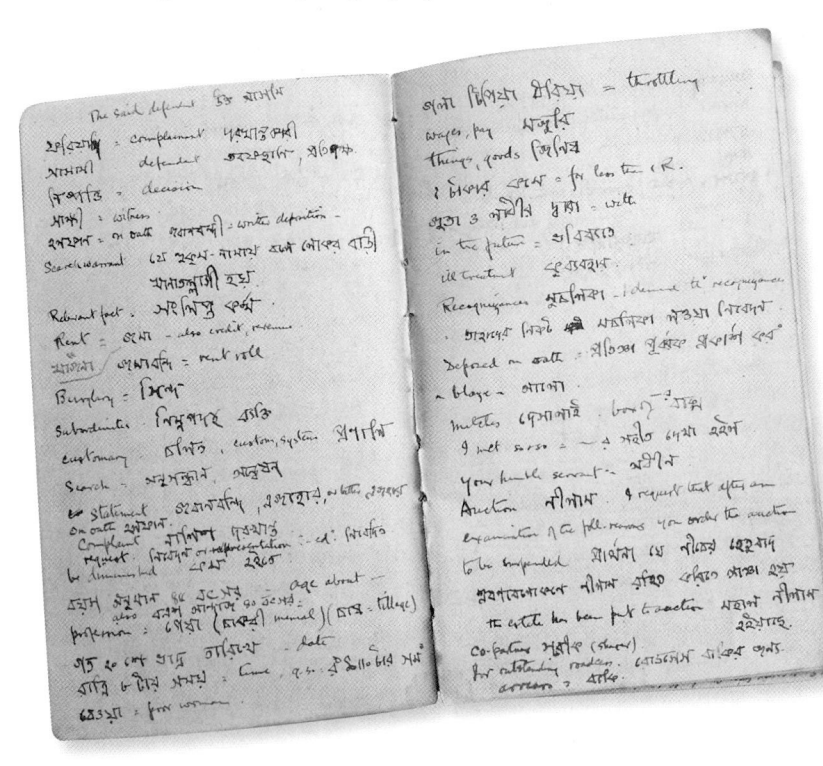

Left: Pages from Ralph's commonplace book. His entries are translations into the vernacular of words and phrases that he is likely to have used in the courtroom.

7. Turbulent Times

Calcutta Cathedral where Ralph was a regular worshipper.

gunfight with police ensued. Two of the assailants died but Dinesh Gupta survived a near-fatal injury and was convicted and sentenced to death.

From April 1931 there was a serious escalation in attacks on British officials, the majority occurring in Bengal. The string of attacks began on 7th April when the District Magistrate of Midnapore, James Peddie, was shot and killed while visiting a school. On 22nd July, a mere five days before Ralph's appointment to hear cases in the Alipore Sessions Court, Sir John Hotson, acting Governor of Bombay, was shot at while visiting a Library in Poona but escaped unharmed. On the same day at a hearing of a gang in the Alipore Court one of the prisoners had suddenly drawn a knife and stabbed two police constables, the Clerk of the Bench and a fellow prisoner. The following day two young British officers were stabbed while asleep on a train bound for Poona, one dying shortly afterwards of his wounds. (The case became known as the Punjab Mail Murder.)

In spite of a strengthened police presence, all British officials must have been acutely aware of the threat to their personal safety as they carried out their public duties. For Ralph, however, there were two additional factors which would have made his situation especially perilous. The first was that he had been president of various tribunals, including the trial of Dinesh Gupta who had been one of the two murderers of Lieutenant-General Simpson in December 1930 (for which he had been hanged); his fellow revolutionaries might seek to revenge his death. The second, and this may or may not be related to the sentencing of Dinesh Gupta, was that Ralph had been receiving threatening letters for several days, as a result of which a special guard had been posted at his home in Calcutta which he shared with his wife and daughter. But would even this heightened level of protection both at home and in court be sufficient?

Chapter 8

Lethal Encounter

On Monday 27th July Ralph was hearing cases in his court at Alipore, a court which was not unfamiliar with acts of violence. The hearings of the *Alipore Bomb Case* had been held there in 1908 and only five days earlier a prisoner had attacked court officials with a knife. On the face of it he appears to have been well-guarded with two sergeants and two constables in attendance, although it is unclear as to where exactly each was positioned.

The entrance to the Courthouse at Alipore.

The trial room, Alipore Sessions Court.

He was about to resume the sitting after lunch when from the public area at the far end of the courtroom a Bengali revolutionary, later identified as Bismal Gupta who had connections with the Bengali Revolutionary Party, drew a Colt revolver and fired at Ralph. The shot missed him but Gupta then rushed to the adjacent witness box and shot Ralph in the head. One of the constables who was stationed outside rushed in and was shot and wounded. As the murderer tried to escape he was shot dead by one of the police sergeants at the entrance to the court. Ralph was taken immediately to the Presidency Hospital in Calcutta where he was pronounced dead.

A letter was found in Bismal Gupta's pocket which read in Bengali: *"Be thou destroyed. This is the reward for the injustice done to Dinesh Gupta –*

8. Lethal Encounter

(Signed) *Bismal Gupta.*" This suggests that the likely motive for the murder was Ralph's role in the sentencing of Dinesh Gupta for the killing of Lieutenant-General Simpson in December 1930. It is also possible that Ralph's assassin was the Bismal Das Gupta who was wanted in connection with the murder of District Magistrate James Peddie in April 1931.[21]

The first public response to the murder came within minutes when the Bengal Legislative Council, on meeting at three o'clock that afternoon, adjourned as a mark of respect. The following day the flags on all public buildings in Calcutta were flown at half-mast. A Reuters telegram from Calcutta alerted the British press to the tragedy within hours, enabling several provincial evening newspapers to break the story. One of the first was the *Dundee Evening Telegraph* whose headline – "JUDGE MURDERED IN CALCUTTA COURT" – was spread across the whole of the top of page 4. *The Shields Daily News* which covered the Tynemouth and Whitley Bay area also carried it, though as their lead story, under multiple headlines: *"Another Murder in India"* | *"Judge Assassinated in Court"* | *"Mr Ralph Garlick Murdered"* | *"Fourth Outrage that has taken place this Month."*

The next day, Tuesday 28th, *The Times* was the most prominent of the national dailies to feature the story, which it did with two items. The first was a *"Report from Our Correspondent in Calcutta"* under the headline *"British Murdered Judge"*. The report fleshed out Reuter's earlier account, alluding to Ralph's widow and daughter in Calcutta and his two sons at school in Cheltenham, describing him as *"a popular officer, friendly with all communities, and a good Judge,"* and concluding with the observation that *"feeling in Calcutta is strong."* This was followed a few pages further on with Ralph's 340-word Obituary.

Most of the newspapers, both national and provincial, went over pretty well the same ground in their accounts of the murder, but one of the nationals, *The Daily Herald* in its 28th July edition, offered a clue as to how the killer was able to gain entry to an ostensibly secure courtroom in the first instance: *"Armed police were stationed at the Court but while the police sergeant was at lunch the assailant walked in."* Whether Gupta had familiarized himself with the protection officers' lunch routine as part of his planning or whether it was a chance entry will never be known.

Provincial newspapers in all four quarters of the UK ran the syndicated story in the days following the murder, each shaping it to suit their particular needs and either trimming or augmenting it to fit the available column inches.

Ralph Garlic

Phrases such as *"Terrorist Outrage"*, *"Judge Murdered in Court"*, *"Dastardly Crime"* appeared frequently as headlines and set the tone of the reports that followed. A few of the provincials were able to establish a connection with the Garlick family. The *Northampton Mercury*, for example, pointed out that Ralph was the grandson of George Garlick Senior who had been the headmaster of the British School at Daventry many years before. The *Western Mail*, on the other hand, under the title *"His Associations with Swansea"* reported that Ralph and Daisy had lived for some time at Trenarth, Mumbles and that she was the daughter of Colonel Charles of Swansea.

The murder animated the House of Commons. The Secretary of State for India, Mr William Wedgwood Benn,[22] was asked to make a statement to the House about Ralph's murder. Mr Benn replied:

> *"I have just received the following telegram from the Government of Bengal. 'Regret to have to report that Garlick, Sessions Judge, Alipore, was shot dead today in Court, by assassin, at present unknown, who was himself killed by guard.' The House will, I am sure, desire to express its sincere sympathy with the relatives of this officer."*

Ralph's Death Certificate. Cause of death is given as "Bullet wound" (column 8).

8. Lethal Encounter

Mr Benn was questioned further by MPs who clearly shared the view of many on the ground in India that the Government was not doing enough to *"prevent incitement to murder in the Press and at public meetings."* Mr Benn offered little in the way of reassurance, saying only that *"action was taken where necessary and the Government were fully alive to their responsibility for the safety of their officials."*

In India Mr Benn's statement did little to quell the anger that had been roused among all communities. The correspondent of *The Morning Post* and *The Scotsman* reported that:

> *"The outrage has aroused intense feeling among Europeans and moderate Indians in Calcutta, and the atmosphere this evening suggests a popular outburst is near. The series of cowardly murders of defenceless men doing their administration work ... have induced a tremendous reaction against the official policy of leniency to lawbreakers, which a few months ago was accepted with resignation."*

"The atmosphere this evening," was a reference to a protest meeting that was held in Calcutta's Dalhousie Institute, one of its largest buildings, the numbers attending being so great that many had to remain outside. Representatives of the various communities gave speeches, their drift being that the Government was *"spineless"* for failing to deal with open incitement to violence. There was condemnation of Ralph's *"callous murder ... while carrying out the duties of his office"* and the Government was urged *"to use all the powers at its disposal to crush the growing menace of anarchism in this country."* Several resolutions were passed by the meeting which were telegraphed to the Prime Minister Ramsay MacDonald and other political leaders. These included Winston Churchill who was fiercely opposed to British Government policy on India which he famously described as that of trying to placate the Indian tiger with cat's meat.

The Bengal Legislative Council passed a resolution condemning the murder and its President, the Hon. the Raja of Santosh, issued a personal statement:

> *"I am really shocked to hear of this dastardly crime because Mr Garlick was personally known to me. It is a deplorable thing that a public servant of Mr Garlick's reputation should die while doing his duty, and in a manner which would grieve all reasonable men."*

Ralph Garlic

A day earlier Muslim leaders, who had gathered in Simla to discuss matters affecting their own community, had been shocked by the news of Ralph's murder and added their voice to the condemnations:

> *"By reason of his long service to India, his work on Special Tribunals, and his personal fearlessness, Mr Garlick was well-known far beyond the Province in which he met his death."*

The Muslim leaders went on to issue a statement in which they placed on record *"their abhorrence at the recent murderous outrages committed on faithful servants of the country,"* and urged *"all sincerely patriotic citizens to do everything to purge the country of this stain on its name."*

The Indian press was also roused. Under the headline *"A Murder has been Arranged"* the *Statesman* newspaper dealt first with Ralph's assassination before going on to make a remarkable attack on the Indian National Congress, accusing its leaders of encouraging violence and asserting that it *"has shown itself unworthy of controlling the destinies of India."*

Not all was sound and fury, however. Elsewhere in India the response to Ralph's murder was less strident. In Dacca, for example, where Ralph had been a judge, the law courts and educational institutions were closed on 29th July as a mark of respect.

By Thursday 30th the dust had settled sufficiently for *The Times* to publish a eulogy for Ralph. Although penned by *"a correspondent"* it was clearly the work of someone who knew him well in India, probably a fellow member of the judiciary:

> *"Mr R.R. Garlick, who was murdered by a Bengali assassin in his Court Room at Alipore, Calcutta, was one of those exceptional men whose range of powers and charm was severely limited by the additional characteristics of a genuine and almost morbid self-deprecation and by a conscience so urgent that it rarely allowed him respite from official work for the enjoyment even of the most ordinary social pleasures. But until increasing deafness added to his natural shyness, no one was a more delightful companion or one whose presence at social gatherings, always difficult to secure, was more eagerly sought for. His sympathies were so broad that it could be truly said of him: 'nihil humanum a me alienum puto.'*[23] *The breadth of his knowledge was astonishing, and in everything he wrote or said, even amid the cumbrous mass of a District Judge's*

8. Lethal Encounter

work, there was manifest that delicacy of touch and phrase which marked a finely tempered scholar's mind. He illustrated the truth of Lord Macmillan's recent saying that the judicial mind gains in poise and finish by refreshing itself ever anew with what is best in literature.

As a Judge, his overriding desire to do justice and to hear everything out, his horror of short cuts and summary decisions, imposed on him the necessity of working long hours in order to keep abreast of his file, and his methods sometimes gave his work the appearance of lacking incisiveness. The standard of his legal knowledge was, however, high, and only his deafness, of which his own tendency to self-depreciation led him not to make too much, prevented his promotion to the High Court Bench at a time when his industry and abilities were generally recognized to be inferior to those of none in Bengal."

Two other members of the Garlick family featured in the press that week. Helen Perkin was the daughter of Ralph's sister Gertrude (Nell) who had been killed in a motor accident near Shipston-on-Stour in 1925. Helen, following in the family's music tradition, was a promising pianist who had recently broadcast on the BBC some works specially written for her by John Ireland. Interviewed by the press she confirmed that her uncle had been receiving threatening letters in connection with cases he had tried but that he was resolved to carry on with his work. She also confirmed that he had just decided to apply for leave preparatory to retirement, and would have been coming home soon.

The second Garlick to feature was Ralph's younger brother Charles. Described as *"late of 45 Wood Street, Stratford-upon-Avon, piano tuner and dealer in music and musical instruments"*, the London Gazette formally announced Charles's bankruptcy in its 29th July edition. Thus ended the sixty-years long association of the Garlick music business with the town. The timing of its demise was extraordinary, coinciding as it did with Ralph's murder.

Chapter 9

Depart with Honour

While Ralph's slaying caused shock in many quarters, both Indian and English, by far its greatest impact would have been upon his widow and daughter in Calcutta. That twenty-year-old Helena's hair turned white almost overnight was a singular manifestation of its effect. The ladies had little time for private reflection, however, as Ralph's funeral was held the next day, a motorised cortege making its way to Calcutta Crematorium, the lead vehicle bearing Ralph's coffin on top of which lay a cross of red roses and a wreath of lilies from Daisy and Helena. The service was conducted by the Bishop of Calcutta and the Governor of Bengal was represented by Colonel W.A.K. Fraser. The large congregation was drawn from all sections of the community, European and Indian. In the course of the next few weeks Daisy and Helena were fully engaged in winding up the family's affairs in India, saying farewell to friends, and packing their belongings in preparation for their departure for England.

The first Stratfordians to be alerted to the dreadful happening in India were Ralph's older sister Elsie and her headmaster husband William. It was to the Howe's home at Grove House School in Greenhill Street that the shock-inducing telegram was sent. The message was blunt:

"Regret have to report that Garlick was shot dead in Court today. Bengal."

Given the prominence of the Howes and the wider Garlick family in the town it is no surprise that (according to the *Stratford-upon-Avon Herald*) news of the tragedy was known throughout Stratford by the following morning (Tuesday 28th). The Howes must have shown enormous resilience because that

9. Depart with Honour

afternoon they fulfilled the duties required of them as headmaster and wife to act as hosts at the school's Annual Sports Day, attending on guests, presenting prizes and making speeches. As it turned out the most important guest present at the Sports was the Mayor of Stratford, Councillor Robert Smith, for whom the news about Ralph would have been a cause of particular anguish.

A childhood friend and contemporary of Ralph's at King Edward VI School, Robert Mansell Smith had never left Stratford but remained to make his own mark on the town's affairs. He was first elected mayor in 1921 when, concerned about the widespread poverty and distress in the town caused mainly by rising unemployment, he founded the Mayor's Fund which functions to this day, providing financial assistance to local, needy senior citizens by way of its grocery voucher scheme. Given his long association with Ralph, his attendance in his capacity as civic leader at the two memorial services held in Stratford would have been especially poignant.

By the end of Tuesday it is most unlikely that there was anybody in the town, newspaper reader or not, who was not aware of the tragic event in India. However, it was not until the following Friday, its designated publishing day, that Stratfordians were able to read a full account of it in their own newspaper, the *Stratford-upon-Avon Herald*. Unsurprisingly, it appeared on the front page as the leading article and ran to one and a half columns of print. Compared to virtually all the provincial papers which had run the story earlier that week, the *Herald's* headline was fairly restrained: "Stratford Man Murdered / Well-known Indian Judge." It began by rehearsing the details of the killing and the responses to it both in India and the House of Commons. The article went on to trace Ralph's career at King Edward VI School, at Pembroke College, and in the ICS, relating that on his last visit to Stratford he had opened a garden party at Grove House in aid of Medical Missions and made several references to India in his speech.

There followed *"A Mayoral Appreciation"* in which Robert Smith spoke of his friend's *"sterling and generous character (which) made him exceedingly popular among his school fellows,"* of how *"his mental attainments enabled him to secure a high place in his classes,"* qualities which *"were taken by him into the larger world outside."* In speaking of Ralph's honesty and sense of duty the Mayor quoted extracts from a letter which he had received from Ralph in reply to a congratulatory note which he had sent on his appointment to the High Court of Calcutta two years earlier. Ralph had written of how he took pleasure from *"the approbation of the friends of one's childhood,"* and from *"the*

Ralph's funeral cortege in Calcutta.

good opinion of one's native town," yet doubted that he had done much in his life to help his *"fellow-men."* Naturally Robert Smith took the contrary view, asserting that: *"Earnest, honest, faithful to his convictions, he influenced others for good by the silent eloquence of his life."*

The *Stratford-upon-Avon Herald* followed up its lead story with a second item on an inside page in which an anonymous writer, under the heading *"An Empire Builder,"* reflected on how the news of Ralph's murder *"was received with consternation, if not with absolute disbelief,"* in the town. He mused that Stratford was a *"quiet spot, the world passes by, and we seem to be spectators rather than players. To connect our quiet town with the momentous happenings in India seemed almost absurd, and that a Stratfordian should be murdered was incredible."*

Stratfordians had their first opportunity to pay their respects in person the next day when a Memorial Service was held at the Congregational Church in Rother Street. As it was not a burial the service was stripped of a funeral atmosphere and was conducted rather as a tribute to *"a martyr on duty"*; as an appreciation of a life's work nobly done; and as an expression of homage to someone who had brought honour upon his town. The Church, of course, had been the Garlick family's place of worship for the previous seventy years and in spite of his thirty years abroad Ralph had continued to regard it as his spiritual home. His relatives, friends and members of the Church were present in number. As it had been designated a civic occasion, the Mayor, aldermen and councillors walked from the Town Hall preceded by the Town Beadle and mace-bearers, while the Stratford police formed a guard of honour. A sizeable contingent of Old Boys (including several of Ralph's contemporaries) and present members of King Edward VI School were led by the headmaster, the Rev. Cecil Knight. The service was conducted by the minister, the Rev. R. Goodfield, who spoke of Ralph's courage:

"He dispensed justice knowing it would be misunderstood and that an assassin's hand would be raised against him, but the warning did not turn him from the path he had chosen for himself. There were certain things impossible to him. He could not be cruel or inhuman. He was fair-minded and civil to contrary opinions, yet when duty demanded the exercise of justice he went straight forward without fearing danger."

The Mayor, who had lost a lifelong friend, read a passage from Ecclesiasticus which began most appropriately with the words: *"Let us now praise famous men."* The Mayor later disclosed that he had received a telegram from the Secretary of State for India (Mr Wedgwood Benn) which read:

"The Secretary of State for India desires to associate himself with the public manifestation of sorrow and sympathy."

Accompanying the Mayor in his procession to the Church was Sir Basanta Mullick, a member of the Council of India, who was representing the Secretary of State for India. In an interview following the service Sir Basanta, who had also been a High Court Judge in Bengal when he met Ralph, said:

"He was loved by everyone, and he left a great mark on the (Indian Civil) Service. He was a man of very genuine character and sincerity of purpose."

In India, meanwhile, some of the country's most influential nationalist leaders were speaking out against the spate of political murders. In an issue of his publication *"Young India"* Gandhi condemned Ralph's murder, asserting *"that every act of political violence injured the non-violent movement."* Pandit

Nehru, a former president of the Indian National Congress and the future first Prime Minister of India, declared that *"it was essential for the Congress to regret and discountenance any attempt at violence."*

The Homecoming

The journey home for Daisy and Helena, accompanied by the urn containing Ralph's ashes, will have been a sorrowful one. They travelled by train across India before embarking on the P&O vessel *Ranchi* at Bombay and arrived in England on 28th August. They journeyed on to Stratford to stay with Elsie and William Howe at Grove House, where they were reunited with the two boys, George and John.

Ralph's funeral service was held at Holy Trinity Church on 2nd September, the very Church to which Ralph had walked with such pride at the head of his school fellows forty-eight years earlier at the first Shakespeare Birthday procession. Daisy and her three children were supported by a great many family and friends. Robert Smith as Mayor was in attendance once again, accompanied by several councillors and, *"a number of prominent residents."* Several clergymen participated in the service, including two who had known Ralph in India. The Rev. Sir Nicholas Beatson Bell, who gave a reading, was a former Governor of Assam but was now vicar of Fritwell, Oxfordshire, and had known Ralph for practically the whole of his thirty years in India. After the service, Sir Nicholas spoke warmly of Ralph's kindness and consideration to his subordinates and his fairness in his judicial capacity; and about how he was extremely modest about himself and was highly principled in every way.

The second clergyman from India was the Rev. Cyril Pearson who was chaplain of Calcutta Cathedral where Ralph had worshipped, and had known him since 1916. He said of Ralph that his outstanding characteristic was extraordinary gentleness and sympathy towards the Indian people. Both men emphasized that Ralph was a man rightly held in the highest respect by British and Indian alike.

To organ accompaniment the clergy met the funeral cortege at the West door. The urn containing Ralph's ashes was enclosed within a casket made of teak and bore the inscription: *"The ashes of the late Ralph Reynolds Garlick, aged 55 years. 'Thy Will be Done'"*. The casket rested on a flower-decked bier.

The hymns and readings were fitting for the occasion (*"Now upon the farther shore lands the voyager at last"*/ *"O valiant hearts"*). At the end of the service the choir conducted the bier to the West door, from where the funeral cortege proceeded to the cemetery in Evesham Road. Here, at his parents' grave, the Rev. Pearson conducted the committal. A memorial stone was later placed on the grave, one that was already shared with Ralph's sister Nell Perkin who had been killed in the motor accident six years earlier. The memorial reads:

"IN LOVING MEMORY OF THEIR SON
RALPH REYNOLDS GARLICK
A BARRISTER-AT-LAW
INDIAN CIVIL SERVICE, BENGAL
SENIOR DISTRICT AND SESSIONS JUDGE
DIED WHILE SERVING HIS COUNTRY
CALCUTTA JULY 27 1931
REQUESTCAT IN PACE"

~ ~ ~

The Garlick family grave at the Evesham Road Cemetery in Stratford; Ralph's commemorative stone is at the forepart.

Ralph's stone memorial, Evesham Road Cemetery.

9. Depart with Honour

Family Fortunes

Daisy's return to England was permanent and she and Helena obtained a flat in Cheltenham. (Daisy remained in Cheltenham for the remainder of her life, barring occasional visits abroad). George was now in his final year at Cheltenham College but John still had four more years ahead of him. Their circumstances were now rather more straitened than they had been in India, and Helena felt obliged to learn dressmaking. She was married in Shanghai Cathedral in 1936 but left for Canada shortly before it was occupied by the Japanese in 1941. (Her husband, who had remained behind, was interned in a Japanese camp). Helena returned to Shanghai after the war and was there when the communists took control in 1949. She died in Colchester in 2000.

Ralph and Daisy's oldest son George went to the Royal Military Academy Sandhurst after leaving Cheltenham College, and in 1933 was posted to the 13th Duke of Connaught's Own Lancers, Indian Army, as a second lieutenant. He was in the last cavalry charge in the North-West Frontier (now Afghanistan). At the outbreak of the Second World War his regiment was converted from Horse to Tanks. He served in North Africa, where he saw action at El Alamein and at the recapture of Tobruk, and was awarded the Military Cross. After the Germans were driven out of North Africa George's regiment was sent to Italy, then to India, and finally to Burma. By the end of the war he was an acting Lieutenant Colonel and second in command of the Regiment (and the holder of campaign and gallantry medals). After the war he emigrated to Tanganyika where he built up a very successful mixed farming enterprise of approximately 4,000 acres. He returned to the United Kingdom in 1961 shortly after Tanganyika gained independence as Tanzania, but emigrated to Zimbabwe in 1964 and died there in 1986.

John Garlick also embarked on a military career after leaving Cheltenham in 1935. He joined the Royal Military Academy Woolwich and on gaining his commission joined the Royal Corps of Signals. He served with the Corps for the duration of the War and held the rank of Captain at its end. John did not marry but lived with Daisy in Cheltenham, where he was employed at the Government Communications Headquarters (GCHQ). The fact that he spoke Russian must have been significant, but he never spoke about the nature of the work in which he was engaged. He died in Cheltenham in 1986.

George Garlick had a successful military career.

9. Depart with Honour

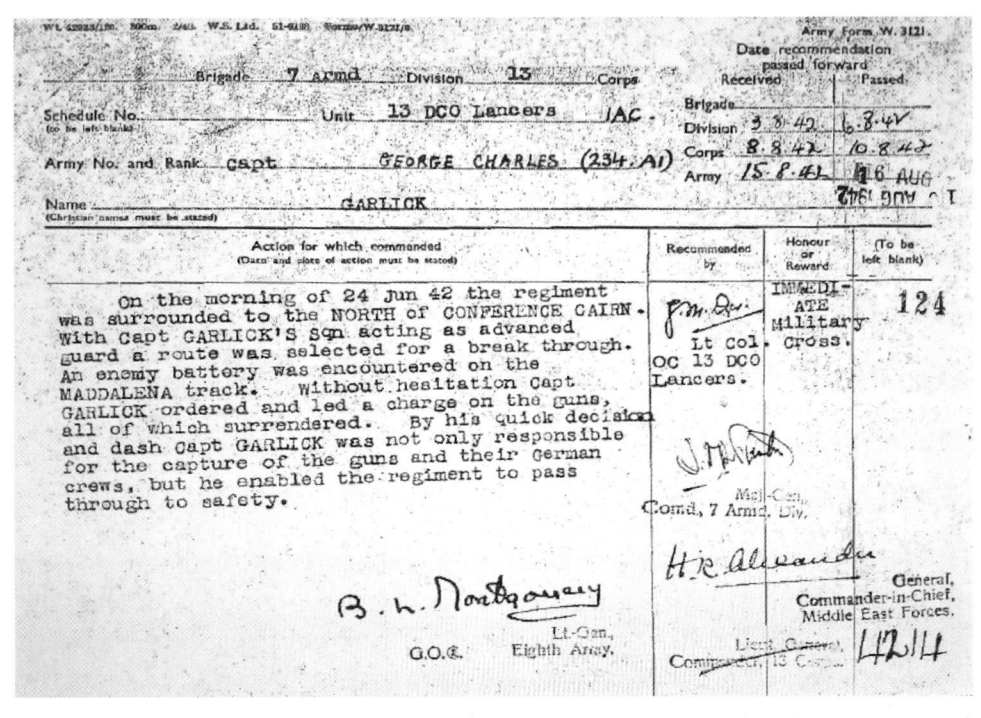

George Garlick's recommendation for a Military Cross. The last two signatures are those of General Montgomery, GOC Eighth Army, and General Alexander, Commander in Chief, Middle East Forces.

George Garlick served on the North-West Frontier.

Helena Garlick, probably at the time of her marriage in 1936.

Chapter 10

Remembrance

In late 1933 the King Edward VI Old Boys' Association set up the *Garlick Memorial Fund*, with the ubiquitous Robert Mansell Smith as its chairman and treasurer, to pay for a tablet in Ralph's memory, any surplus to be used to fund a scholastic prize. The fund was well supported, enabling the purchase of a fine bronze tablet set on an oak base which was unveiled with due ceremony at the School on Saturday 28th June 1934 by the Master of the Rolls and High Steward of the Borough of Stratford, Lord Hanworth. Members of the Garlick family present included Daisy and her daughter Helena and son John, together with Ralph's brother Charles and two sisters Elsie and Elizabeth and their husbands. Some of Ralph's friends and colleagues from India were there to pay their respects: Sir Herbert Cuming (High Court Judge, Calcutta) and Lady Cuming, Mr O'Sullivan (late Inspector of Indian Police), Mr and Mrs Leeson (Calcutta), and Mr T. Baboneau (late Indian Civil Service). Local dignitaries included Sir Archie and Lady Flower, the Mayoress (Mrs J.H. Rowe), and Vicar of the Collegiate Church the Rev. Canon Melville. Many Old Boys gave their support, including the Association's chairman Mr H. Carr-Smith and Fund chairman Robert Smith. Apologies were received from, among others, Lord Halifax, (who, as Lord Irwin, had been Viceroy of India 1926-31) and Anthony Eden (MP for Warwick and Lord Privy Seal).

With the tablet affixed to the wall in Big School and covered by the Union flag the Headmaster the Rev. Cecil Knight opened proceedings by affirming that the tablet was part of a two-fold memorial; the other part was the creation of a fund to provide a sum of money annually for a prize, to be known as the *Ralph Garlick Memorial Gift,* which would be awarded each year to the boy proceeding to a place of higher education to enable him to purchase books or equipment. The Headmaster encapsulated the honour which Ralph had *"won for himself and brought no less to his old School"* by quoting *"that other Old Boy who, more than three hundred years ago, sat in this very room"*:

"He hath borne his faculties so meek, hath been so clear in his great office."[24]

Lord Hanworth then spoke of how grammar and public schools infused those who attended them with a great sense of *"loyalty"*, a loyalty to their school, its system and traditions; and a loyalty to the country and their King. It was fitting that a memorial to Ralph should be raised in the school where his character was formed and which by his subsequent life he honoured. Those present, Lord Hanworth continued, were paying tribute to a man who was cut off in the prime of his life while fulfilling his duty fearlessly, for there was no question that he was a marked man, having had many indications that his work brought daily anxieties and dangers.

Lord Hanworth then drew aside the Union flag covering the tablet which bears the following inscription in Old Roman lettering:

"To the memory of Ralph Reynolds Garlick, Senior District and Sessions Judge, Bengal, sometime a member of this School and Scholar of Pembroke College, Oxford. Noble in character, modest in bearing, faithful and just in his great office, honoured by all, he died at the post of duty by the hand of an assassin, at Alipore, July 27th 1931. This tablet was erected by his many friends in the school and town."

At the foot of the tablet, which was created by a local craftsman,[25] appear the Town arms and the Star of India, and at the top the School badge and motto, *"Age quod agis."*

The memorial was then dedicated by Canon Melville, who included in the prayer he had composed for the occasion the words: *"grant that all who shall see it here may follow his example of industry, integrity, and uprightness."*

~ ~ ~

The memorial tablet has ensured Ralph Garlick's posthumous standing among the School's more illustrious Old Boys. It has recently been refurbished and relocated to the corridor at the entrance to Pedagogue's House. The Garlick name retains a presence in Big School, however. As Head Boy between 1892 and 1894 his is the first name to appear on the Honours Board which hangs on its northern wall. Thus Ralph Garlick has the unique distinction among Old Edwardians of having both his scholar's life honoured and his death commemorated within the precincts of the school.

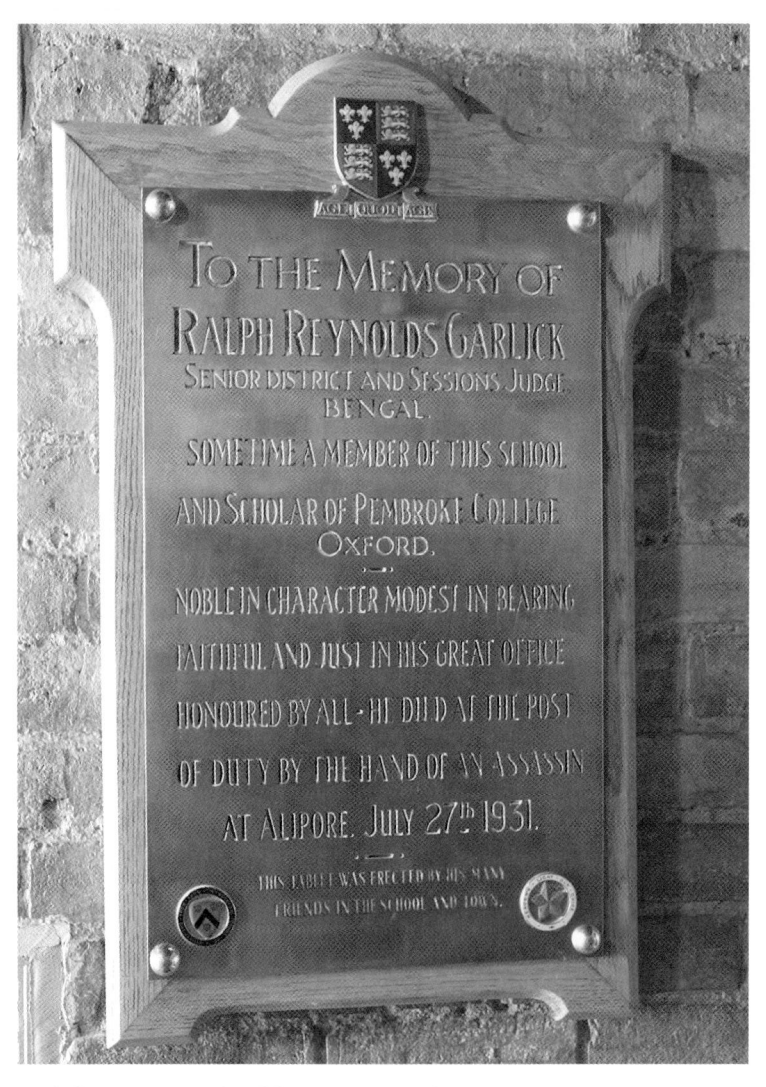

Ralph's Memorial tablet at its new location in K.E.S.
[By kind permission of Mrs Susan Swann].

Garlick Family Tree

(Abbreviated – includes only those mentioned in text)

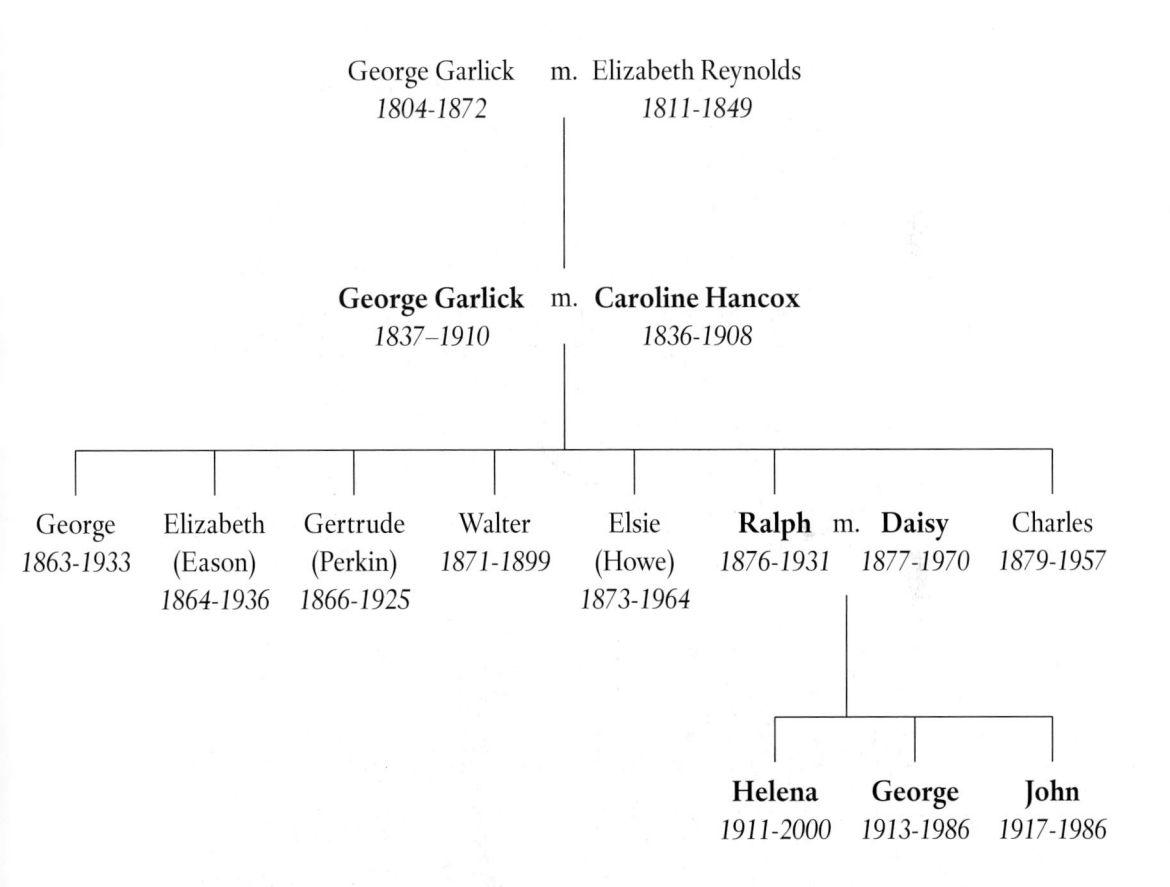

George Garlick   m.   Elizabeth Reynolds
1804-1872   *1811-1849*

George Garlick   m.   **Caroline Hancox**
1837–1910   *1836-1908*

George	Elizabeth (Eason)	Gertrude (Perkin)	Walter	Elsie (Howe)	**Ralph**	m.	**Daisy**	Charles
1863-1933	*1864-1936*	*1866-1925*	*1871-1899*	*1873-1964*	*1876-1931*		*1877-1970*	*1879-1957*

Helena	**George**	**John**
1911-2000	*1913-1986*	*1917-1986*

Notes and References

1. British Schools were chiefly under Nonconformist auspices, in contrast to National Schools which were under Church of England patronage. Many of the leading burgesses of Stratford were educated at the British School in Rother Street.
2. No 45 Wood Street is now (2019) *Caffe Vineria,* an Italian restaurant.
3. Quoted in Bearman, *Stratford-upon-Avon. A History of its Streets and Buildings.*
4. Quoted in Forrest, *The Old Houses of Stratford-upon-Avon.*
5. William Howe was the leader of the Choral Society's own orchestral section. He was also a member of the Shakespeare Birthday Celebration Committee until well into his eighties.
6. Quoted in Brownhill, *An Illustrated History of the Stratford-upon-Avon Choral Society.*
7. Although there were no fatalities on the Avon at Stratford during the Great Frost, two young men drowned at Warwick and a boy at Evesham. However, at Stratford a youth fell through thin ice under the Clopton Bridge while playing hockey but with the assistance of skaters and the use of a ladder he was pulled from the water, *"apparently little the worse for his immersion."*
8. Quoted in Boswell, *The Life of Samuel Johnson.*
9. Quoted in Rogers, *The Samuel Johnson Encyclopedia.*
10. Morpheus: god of sleep or of dreams.
11. *The Ossianic Poems:* A cycle of poems which the Scottish poet James Macpherson (1736-1796) claimed to have translated from the Gaelic language. The authenticity of the translations was challenged by, among others, Samuel Johnson, who was convinced that Macpherson was, *"a mountebank, a liar, and a fraud, and that the poems were forgeries."*
12. The King Edward VI School Boat Club was not formed until 1927.
13. *Tubbing* sessions were designed to teach novices how to row.
14. Quoted in Thompson, *Icarus Went East.*

15. Quoted in Gilmour, *Curzon*.
16. Quoted in Smith, *The Indian Civil Service as a Profession*.
17. In Kipling's estimation the ICS was a hard-working body of men who, under extremely challenging conditions, devoted their lives to the welfare of the native population.
18. District Officer was a generic term, the actual job title being (depending on the province) magistrate, collector or deputy commissioner.
19. The frequency of home furlough for officials had improved markedly since the early nineteenth century. In 1828 Robert Montgomery, grandfather of Field Marshal Viscount Montgomery of Alamein, arrived in India to begin his duties with the Bengal Civil Service and did not return to England, except for one visit, for nearly forty years.
20. Both prisoners were released in 1920.
21. That the assassin was Bismal Gupta as stated in the letter found on the body has been questioned in some quarters, in particular in India. The claim is made that the assassin was in fact another revolutionary who pretended to be Bismal Gupta, a wanted man, so that the police would call off their search for him. I have not pursued this line of enquiry but adhered to the newspaper reports at the time which clearly believed the killer to be Bismal Gupta.
22. William Wedgwood Benn, 1st Viscount Stansgate, was the father of Tony Benn and the grandfather of Hilary Benn.
23. *"I consider nothing human to be alien to me."* (Terence).
24. William Shakespeare, *Macbeth*.
25. George Danks (1872-1953) started his working life as an apprentice to his father, a chandelier maker, before turning to brass.

List of Illustrations

1. Big School circa 2006.
2. Memorial tablet to George Garlick.
3. 45 Wood Street, Stratford-upon-Avon circa 1930.
4. Gertrude (Nell) Garlick.
5. Elsie Garlick.
6. Pig Roast on the frozen River Avon 1891.
7. Ralph's entry in the K.E.S. Admissions Register 1894.
8. The Rev. Laffan, Headmaster of K.E.S. 1885-95.
9. Prize Giving 1890.
10. The Guildhall from Scholars Lane circa 1885.
11. The Guildhall from Church Street circa 1894.
12. The Latin Room 1883.
13. The Latin Room circa 1892.
14. Latin Prize bookplate 1886.
15. Prize Giving 1892.
16. Ralph's collection of Prize books.
17. Prize bound book carrying the K.E.S. crest (1).
18. Prize bound book carrying the K.E.S. crest (2).
19. The Council Chamber circa 1898.
20. Ralph's signature on the early seventeenth century oak table.
21. The Old Quad, Pembroke College 1875.
22. Samuel Johnson's rooms, Pembroke College.
23. Ralph in Pembroke College Eight circa 1898.
24. A rowing trophy.
25. Pembroke College students 1898.
26. Burlington House, London. Examination centre for ICS candidates.
27. Ralph's ICS admission card.
28. Ralph's ICS Indenture.

List of Illustrations

29. Ralph's appointment to Bengal.
30. Ralph's ICS Covenant.
31. Map of Bengal.
32. S.S. "City of Nagpur".
33. Ralph's travel trunk.
34. P&O luggage label.
35. An English magistrate in India 1886.
36. Ralph and Daisy circa 1911 (1).
37. Ralph and Daisy circa 1911 (2).
38. Ralph at Tilbury 1911 preparing to board S.S. "Himalaya".
39. Grove House School, Greenhill Street, Stratford-upon-Avon.
40. Gandhi in 1931.
41. Ralph in Stratford-upon-Avon circa 1925.
42. The Bengal Secretariat, the scene of Lt. General Simpson's murder in 1930.
43. Ralph and Daisy circa 1930.
44. Ralph and Helena circa 1929.
45. A poetic letter from Ralph to Helena 1929.
46. Ralph's commonplace book.
47. Calcutta Cathedral.
48. The Courthouse at Alipore.
49. The Courtroom, Alipore.
50. Ralph's Death Certificate.
51. Ralph's funeral cortege, Calcutta.
52. The Garlick family grave, Stratford-upon-Avon.
53. Ralph's stone memorial on the Garlick family grave.
54. George Garlick in uniform.
55. George Garlick's recommendation for a Military Cross.
56. The Northwest Frontier circa 1934.
57. Helena Garlick circa 1936.
58. Ralph Garlick's Memorial tablet in K.E.S.

Bibliography

Allen, Charles, *Plain Tales from the Raj*, Andre Deutsch, 1976
Allen, Charles, *Raj. A Scrapbook of British India*, B.C.A., 1977
Bearman, Robert, *Stratford-upon-Avon. A History of its Streets and Buildings*, Hendon Publishing Co., 1988
Blunt, Edward, *The I.C.S.*, Faber and Faber, 1937
Boswell, James, *The Life of Samuel Johnson, LL.D,* 1791 (1st)
Brockway, Nora, *A History of the Rother Street Congregational Church*, Birmingham, 1960
Brown, Judith, *Modern India,* Oxford University Press, 1994
Brownhill, Diana, *An Illustrated History of the Stratford-upon-Avon Choral Society*, 1985
Dewey, Clive, *Anglo-Indian Attitudes,* The Hambledon Press, 1993
Duckers, Peter, *The British-Indian Army*, Shire Publications, 2003
Forrest, H.E., *The Old Houses of Stratford-upon-Avon*, Methuen, 1925
Gilmour, David, *The Ruling Caste*, John Murray, 2005
Gilmour, David, *The Long Recessional*, John Murray, 2002
Gilmour, David, *Curzon*, 1994
Gilmour, David, *The British in India*, Allen Lane, 2018
Gopal, S., *The Viceroyalty of Lord Irwin*, Oxford University Press, 1957
Griffiths, P.J., *The British in India*, Robert Hale, 1946
Hoda, Nooral, *The Alipore Bomb Case*, Niyogi Books, 2008
Jaggard, Gerald, *Stratford Mosaic*, Christopher Johnson, 1960
Judd, Denis, *The Lion and the Tiger*, Oxford University Press, 2004
Lalvani, Kartar, *The Making of India*, Bloomsbury, 2016
Lawrence, Sir Walter, *The India We Served*, Cassell, 1928
Lee, Sydney, *Stratford-on-Avon*, Seeley & Co., 1885
Macleod, R.D., *Impressions of an Indian Civil Servant*, Witherby, 1938
Maconochie, Evan, *Life in the Indian Civil Service*, Chapman & Hall, 1926

Bibliography

O'Malley, L.S., *The Indian Civil Service 1601-1930*, Routledge, 1931
Pearson, Richard, *King Edward VI School, Stratford-upon-Avon*, Gresham Books, 2008
Reid, Sir Robert, *Years of Change in Bengal and Assam*, Ernest Benn, 1966
Rogers, Pat, *The Samuel Johnson Encyclopedia*, Greenwood Press, 1996
Royle, Trevor, *Last Days of the Raj*, Michael Joseph, 1989
Smith, Vincent, *The Indian Civil Service as a Profession*, Hodges, Figgis & Co., 1903
Spender, Richard, *The Collected Poems*, Sidgewick & Jackson, 1944
Stephens, Ian, *Unmade Journey*, Stacey International, 1977
Stevenson, Richard, *Bengal Tiger and British Lion*, iUniverse, Inc., 2005
Styles, Philip, *The Borough of Stratford-upon-Avon and the Parish of Alveston*, Oxford University Press, 1945
Symonds, Richard, *Oxford and Empire*, St Martin's Press, 1986
Thompson, Herbert, *Icarus Went East*, Lulu, 2013
Watkins, Leslie, *The Story of Shakespeare's School 1853-1953*, The Herald Press, 1953
Wolpert, Stanley, *A New History of India*, Oxford University Press, 1997
Woodruff, Philip, *The Men Who Ruled India. The Guardians*, Jonathan Cape, 1959

~ ~ ~

Stratford-upon-Avon Herald – various issues
The Stratfordian. The Magazine of King Edward VI School – various issues

Acknowledgements

I have been fortunate to have received help from a number of quarters. Two in particular have been pillars of support throughout. Richard Pearson, King Edward VI School Archivist, has given generously of his time, sharing his considerable knowledge of the history of the school, and providing unfettered access to the trove of school records held in the Memorial Library. His support of the project has been wholehearted since its inception.

Dr. Penny Pullan has shown enormous enthusiasm for my excursion into her great grandfather's biography. She has been an invaluable source of information about the Garlick family, especially during the Indian phase of their lives, and has made freely available a great amount of family memorabilia. Photographs from key parts of the archive have illuminated the text appreciably. She is to be further thanked for her kind donation of Ralph's collection of K.E.S. prizes to the Archive (photo page 26).

I have made extensive use of the Shakespeare Birthplace Trust Record Office and owe thanks to the staff for their diligence and forbearance. Several of the principal photographs have been sourced from the S.B.T. archives.

Chapter 5 would have been less substantial had it not been for intelligence on Ralph's undergraduate days provided by Pembroke College Archivist Amanda Ingram. I owe thanks not only for the material which her research skills uncovered but also for her hospitality during a particularly rainy visit.

Other archivists have also made significant contributions at particular stages of the narrative: Rachael Merrison and Katie Barrett at Cheltenham College; Rachael Roberts at Cheltenham Ladies' College; Celia Pilkington at Inner Temple; and Rebecca Leeman at Oxford University Archives.

Perry Mills, Deputy Headmaster (Pastoral) at King Edward VI School, read the manuscript and made some invaluable suggestions, for which I am most grateful.

Acknowledgements

Also at K.E.S., Susan Swan overcame the challenge it presented to produce a fine photograph of the Garlick tablet in its new location.

Dr. Jenny Davidson was responsible for photographing much of the material in my possession and I thank her for deploying her skills to such good effect.

I was able to procure the key photograph of Big School through the willing assistance of Claire Steele, PA to Mr Tony Bird.

The Committee of the Old Edwardians' Association has marked its support for the biography with a generous grant, for which I am most grateful.

Lastly, I wish to thank my wife Clodagh for her continuous support and for her capable handling of the technical and presentational sides of the project.

All photographs, unless acknowledged, are from the King Edward VI School Archive, Pembroke College Archive, Dr. Pullan's collection, or the author's collection.

Author Biography

The author was educated at King Edward VI Grammar School, Lichfield and the University of Manchester. In 1964-65 he taught at a secondary school in Sierra Leone under the auspices of Voluntary Service Overseas prior to taking up the position of account executive with the London-based Unilever Company, Research Bureau Limited. He left the Company in 1967 in order to study for a P.G.S.E. at the University of Birmingham. In September 1968 he was appointed Head of Economics at King Edward VI School, where he was also involved with coaching rugby, athletics, and swimming. He took early retirement in 1993, following which he joined the K.E.S. Games Department as a part-time coach. His final retirement came in 2015, but he continues to be involved with sport at K.E.S. whenever possible. He is the author of *Hewins, Organ Builders of Stratford-upon-Avon 1856-1958* (2017).

Index

Alexander, General, 79
Alipore Bomb Case, 57, 62, 63
Alipore Sessions Court, 57, 63-65, 66
Alscot Park, 12
Amritsar massacre, 58
Aspinall, Alexander, 15
Assam, 52, 57, 75

Baboneau, T., 80
Bancroft Gardens, 10, 18
Beatson Bell, Rev. Sir Nicholas, 75
Beaumont, Francis, 33
Bengal:
   Legislative Council, 65, 67
   Partition of, 52
   Secretariat, 58-59
Bengali Revolutionary Party, 58, 64
Boswell, James, 30, 32, 84
Bow Street Court, 45
British Olympic Association, 16
British Schools, 4, 10, 84
Burke, Edmund, 33
Burlington House, Piccadilly, 43, 45

Calcutta:
   Bishop of, 70
   Cathedral, 61, 75
   Crematorium, 70
   Dalhousie Institute, 67
   High Court, 53, 71
   Presidency Hospital, 64
   Saint John's Church, 51

Carey, W.E., 12
Carr-Smith, H., 80
Charles, Thomas (father-in-law), 52, 66
Cheltenham College, 15, 41, 55, 65, 77
Cheltenham Ladies' College, 55
Churchill, Winston, 67
City of Nagpur (Ellerman Line), 47
Clopton Bridge, 9
Colbourne, Harold, 9, 11
Congregational Church, 4, 7, 10, 73-74
Cuming, Sir Herbert, 80
Curzon, Lord, 40

Dacca, 68
Daily Herald, 65
Danks, George, 85
Daventry, 66
de Stael, Madame, 32
Deer, Aubrey, 3
Disraeli, Benjamin, 40
District Officer, 48-51, 85
Dyer, Brigadier-General, 58

East India Company, 40, 56
Eden, Anthony, 80
El Alamein, Battle of, 77
Evesham Road Cemetery, 5, 7, 76

Fletcher, John, 33
Flower, Charles, 13
Flower, Sir Archibald, 80
Fraser, Colonel W.A.K., 70

Gandhi, Mohandas, 58, 74
Garlick:
  Caroline (mother), 3, 4, 76
  Charles (brother), 5-7, 13, 55, 69, 80
  Daisy (wife), 51-53, 55, 60, 70, 75, 77, 80
  Elizabeth (sister), 7, 80
  Elsie (sister), 7, 70, 75, 80
  George (grandfather), 66
  George (father), 3-7, 13, 29, 76
  George (brother), 5
  George (son), 55, 75, 77-79
  Gertrude (sister) 7, 69, 76
  Helena (daughter), 53, 55, 60, 70, 75, 77, 79, 80
  John (son), 55, 75, 77
  Lucianne (aunt), 13
  Mary (aunt), 3, 4
  Walter (brother), 5, 11
Garrick, David, 32
Garrick Inn, 9
Goodfield, Rev. R., 59, 74
GCHQ, 77
Greene, Rev., 12
Grove House, 7, 55, 70-71, 75
Guild Chapel, 16
Gupta, Bismal, 64, 85
Gupta, Dinesh, 62, 64-65

Haileybury College, 40
Halifax, Lord, 80

Hancox, George and Harriet (grandparents), 3, 10
Hanworth, Lord, 80-81
Hathway, Richard, 15
Headmasters' Conference, 16
Himalaya (P&O), 53
Holy Trinity Church, 22, 75
Hotson, Sir John, 62
House of Commons, 66, 71
Howe, William (brother-in-law), 7, 55, 70, 75, 84
Hunt, Simon, 30

Indian:
  Army, 39, 57, 77
  Civil Service (ICS), 24, 36, 40-45
  National Congress, 56, 68, 75
  Rebellion 1857/58, 40, 56
Inner Temple, 52
International Olympic Committee, 16
Ireland, John, 69

Jenkins, Thomas, 30
Johnson, Samuel, 30-32, 84

Kelly's Directory, 29
King Edward VI School:
  Archive, 25, 90
  Armoury, 13
  Big School, vii, 13, 19, 80, 82
  Boarding, 12-13
  Boat Club, 84
  Council Chamber, 29
  Delawarr Scholarship, 27
  Examiners, external, 25-28
  Fire Engine, 19

Index

Guild Preparatory School, 12
Guildhall, vii, 18-23
Head Boy, 22, 82
Latin Room, 19
Mathematics Room, 19
Muniment Room, 15
Old Edwardians' Association, 5, 16, 80-81, 91
Pedagogue's House, 18, 82
Plumber's Shop/Sergeant's Lodge, 19
Prize Giving, 16, 17-18, 25-29
School House, 13
Kingsford, District Judge, 57
Kipling, Rudyard, 47, 85
Knight, Rev. Cecil, 74, 80-81

Laffan, Mrs. 13, 22
Laffan, Rev. de Courcy, Ch.2, 22-23, 24-27, 30, 42
Lechlade, 3
Leeson, Mr and Mrs, 80
London Gazette, 69
Lowman, F.J., 58

MacDonald, Ramsay, 67
Macpherson, James, 84
Marylebone Court, 45
Mauritius, 5
Medical Missions, 71
Melville, Rev. Canon, 80-81
Military Cross, 77
Montgomery, Field Marshal, 79, 85
Montgomery, Robert, 85
Morris, William, 36
Mullick, Sir Basanta, 74

National Schools, 84
Nehru, Pandit, 74
New Place, 3, 13
North-West Frontier, 77, 79

Old Bailey, 45
O'Sullivan, Mr., 80
Oxford Local Examinations, 25-26

Page, Frank, 9
Pearson, Rev. Cecil, 75-76
Peddie, James, 62, 65
Pembroke College, Oxford, 27, Ch.5, 45
Perkin, Helen (niece), 69
Persia (SS), 47
Pig Roast (1891), 8-10, 84
Pigott-Smith, Tim, 40
Punjab Mail Murder, 62

Ranchi (P&O), 75
Rawalpindi (P&O), 55
Red Horse Hotel, 9
Reuters, 65
Reynolds, William, 3
"Robinson Fours", 34
Rose, George, 9
Royal Corps of Signals, 77
Rowe, Mrs J.H., 80

Samman, Herbert, 42
Sandhurst, Royal Military Academy, 24, 77
Savage, Richard, 15
Seven Meadows, 18
Shakespeare, William, vii, 3, 13, 30, 32, 33, 81

Shakespeare:
  Birthday Procession, 22, 75
  Birthplace Trust, 15
  Club, 5
  Jubilee (1769), 32
Shipston-on-Stour, 7, 69
Simla, 68
Simpson, Lieutenant-General, 58-59, 62, 65
Smith, Robert Mansell, 8, 71-72, 74, 75, 80
Snitterfield, 3, 10
Statesman, 68
Stratford Boat Club, 33
Stratford Choral Society, 4, 7
Stratford Streets:
  Arden, 9
  Bridge, 9
  Chapel Lane, 13
  Church, 11, 19, 21
  Greenhill, 7, 55, 70-71, 75
  High, 9
  Rother, 4, 7, 10, 73
  Scholars Lane, 20
  West, 3
  Wood, 3-7, 8, 12-13, 55, 69, 84
St. Mary's Lodge, 53
Suez Canal, 47
Swans Nest Hotel, 9
Swansea, 66

Tegart, Charles, 58
Times, 65, 68
Tilbury Dock, 47, 53-54
Torpids, 34
Trinity College, 11
"Tubbing", 33, 84

Viceroy of India, 40, 80
Victoria, Queen, 40

Wedgwood Benn, William, 66-67, 74, 85
West, Master, 12
Wiltshire, Horace, 9
Woolwich, Royal Military Academy, 77
World War One, 57
World War Two, 77